ROCKET

DK

Written by JOSH BARKER

CONTENTS

4	What is a rocket?
6	Under construction
8	Hot-fire testing
10	Rocket fuel
12	Rocket transportation
14	Protecting the payload
16	Super stacking
18	Vehicle Assembly Building
20	Roll to the launch pad
22	Go for launch
24	Blast off!
26	Guidance systems
28	Heat trail
30	Flight path
32	ESA's Ariane
34	Stage separation
36	SpaceX Starship
38	Reusable rockets
40	Soyuz system
42	Long March launch
44	Small launchers
46	Satellite orbits
48	Crewed craft
50	Space Shuttle
52	Docking with the ISS
54	Space Launch System
56	Mighty Saturn V
58	Returning home
60	Launch vehicles
62	Launch sites
64	Index and acknowledgements

LAUNCHING A SATELLITE //
This Atlas V rocket, shown here in 2012 preparing to launch in Florida, USA, carried two NASA satellites into orbit to study radiation surrounding Earth. In 2024, more than 250 rockets were launched around the world, sending 2,695 satellites into orbit. These satellites have a variety of uses, from observing Earth and its climate to flying past neighbouring planets and collecting data about the Universe.

WHAT IS A ROCKET?

A rocket is a vehicle that burns fuel and pushes the exhaust gases out at high speed to create thrust – the force that pushes the rocket into the sky. The rockets in this book are launch vehicles – they carry things into space. Some rockets launch astronauts or uncrewed spacecraft, while others put satellites into orbit.

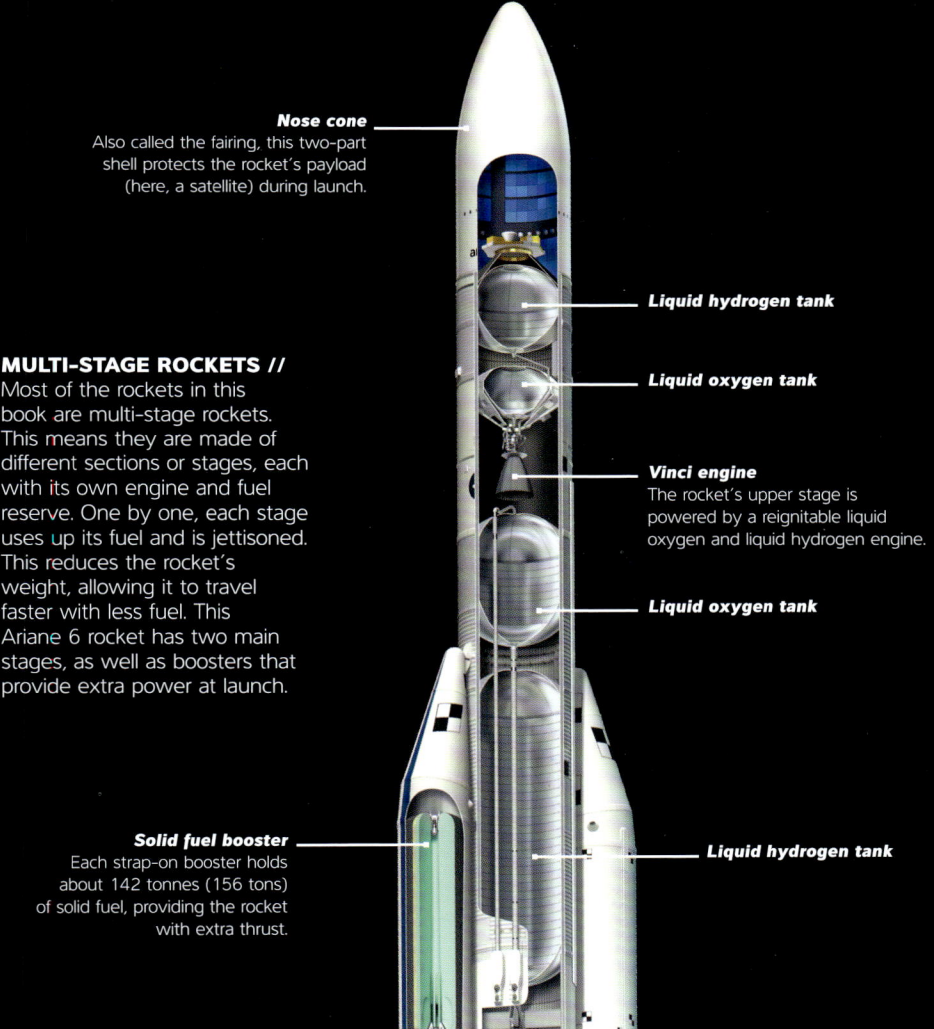

Nose cone
Also called the fairing, this two-part shell protects the rocket's payload (here, a satellite) during launch.

MULTI-STAGE ROCKETS //
Most of the rockets in this book are multi-stage rockets. This means they are made of different sections or stages, each with its own engine and fuel reserve. One by one, each stage uses up its fuel and is jettisoned. This reduces the rocket's weight, allowing it to travel faster with less fuel. This Ariane 6 rocket has two main stages, as well as boosters that provide extra power at launch.

Liquid hydrogen tank

Liquid oxygen tank

Vinci engine
The rocket's upper stage is powered by a reignitable liquid oxygen and liquid hydrogen engine.

Liquid oxygen tank

Solid fuel booster
Each strap-on booster holds about 142 tonnes (156 tons) of solid fuel, providing the rocket with extra thrust.

Liquid hydrogen tank

Vulcain engine
The main stage engine burns liquid oxygen and liquid hydrogen to generate 138 tonnes (152 tons) of thrust.

WHERE DOES SPACE BEGIN? //

There is no set boundary where Earth's atmosphere ends and space begins. Most of the gas in the atmosphere is in the lowest layer, the troposphere. The layers of the atmosphere then get gradually less dense until no gas remains, only the vacuum of space. However most space flight happens at much lower altitudes. Anyone who travels above a point called the Kármán line, 100 km (60 miles) high, is considered an astronaut – a space traveller.

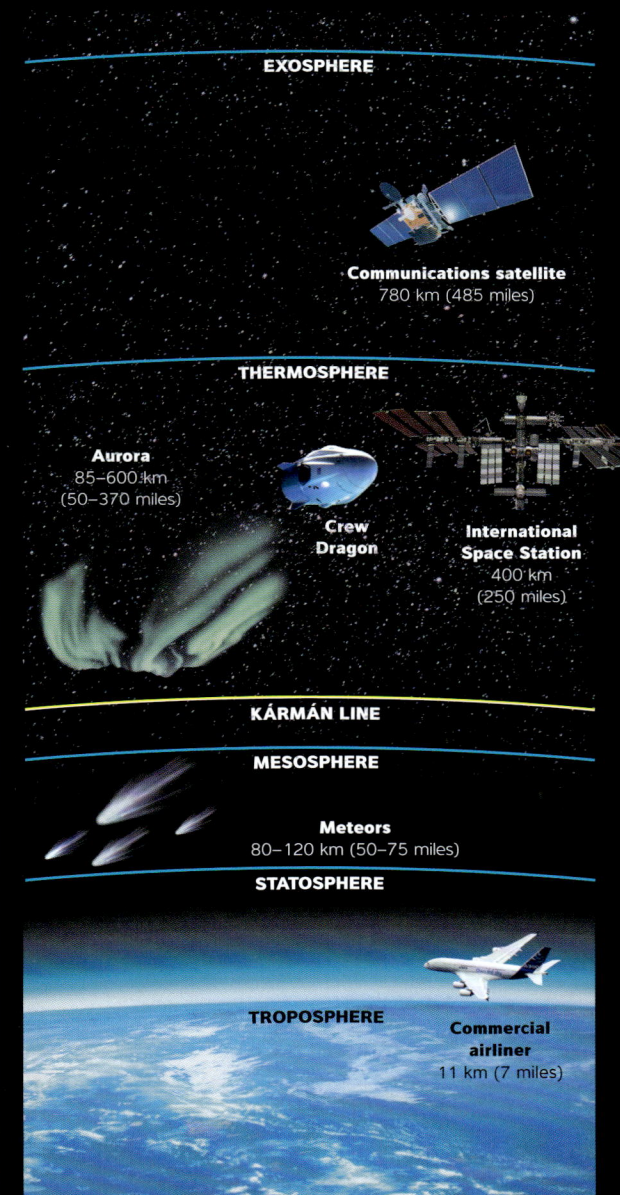

EXOSPHERE

Communications satellite
780 km (485 miles)

THERMOSPHERE

Aurora
85–600 km (50–370 miles)

Crew Dragon

International Space Station
400 km (250 miles)

KÁRMÁN LINE

MESOSPHERE

Meteors
80–120 km (50–75 miles)

STATOSPHERE

TROPOSPHERE

Commercial airliner
11 km (7 miles)

UNDER CONSTRUCTION

Building a rocket requires a huge team of engineers and can take many months. Teams of people carefully plan out the design and building of each component. Each may be made by a different company with specialized facilities. The build must be carried out with the utmost accuracy – even the tiniest mistake could have enormous consequences.

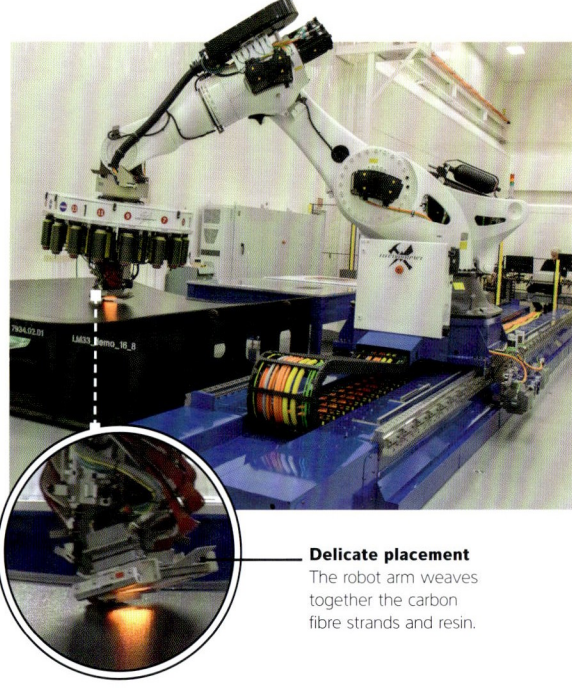

Delicate placement
The robot arm weaves together the carbon fibre strands and resin.

CUTTING THE GRID //
A milling machine shaves a grid pattern into a large metal sheet, which will form the rocket's tank. The rectangular pattern it is carving is called an orthogrid. Using a grid design makes the sheet as thin as possible to reduce weight, while still providing a strong structure that won't bend or collapse.

COMPOSITE MATERIALS //
Some parts of a rocket are made from composite materials. These are precisely engineered by combining two or more materials with different properties. This NASA robot is weaving carbon fibre strands together with resin. The carbon adds strength and the resin adds stiffness.

TESTING //
All rocket components are tested thoroughly. Most testing will be non-destructive – designed to assess a component without destroying it. However, here engineers have deliberately subjected the SLS hydrogen tank to extreme forces to see at which point it does fail.

A HUMAN TOUCH //
A welder works inside the liquid hydrogen tank of NASA's SLS rocket. Part of the enormous rocket's core stage, it is 40 m (130 ft) tall and is made from an alloy of aluminium. Most of the welding is done by machine but small holes that remain are repaired by hand.

HOT-FIRE TESTING

A rocket engine goes through several vital tests before it is used for a rocket launch. First, a series of cold tests check that the fuel flows with no leaks, but without igniting it. Next, the "hot-fire" test checks the engine's performance when the fuel is ignited. When all the tests have been completed, the engine will either be returned to the assembly building for further refinements or made ready for launch.

TEST BUILDING //
This towering plume of smoke billowing from the Naro Space Centre in Goheung, South Korea, is from the final hot-fire test of the Nuri rocket. All four first stage KRE-075 engines are firing as the Korea Aerospace Research Institute (KARI) gets closer to launching the first rocket ever built in South Korea.

READY FOR LAUNCH //
Nuri is a medium-lift launcher, meaning it can carry payloads of up to 3,300 kg (7,275 lb) to low Earth orbit, and it has three stages. During its first test launch in 2021, the rocket didn't reach orbit. After its second test launch in 2022, shown here, it successfully carried a dummy satellite and CubeSats into low Earth orbit.

NURI ROCKET //
At the Naro Space Centre, a single rocket engine is ignited to see how it performs. This is a KRE-075 engine, used for the first and second stages of South Korea's Nuri rocket.

Exhaust smoke
Grey smoke pours from the exhaust of a separate motor powering the pumps that pull fuel into the main combustion chamber (see panel below).

HOW A ROCKET ENGINE WORKS //

There are different kinds of rocket engines but they almost all work by transferring fuel, such as kerosene or liquid hydrogen, and an oxidizer (often liquid oxygen) into a combustion chamber. The explosion that results when these two materials (together called the propellant) mix is powerful enough to boost the rocket out of Earth's atmosphere into space. The KRE-075 engine uses a gas generator to power pumps that pull the propellant into the combustion chamber.

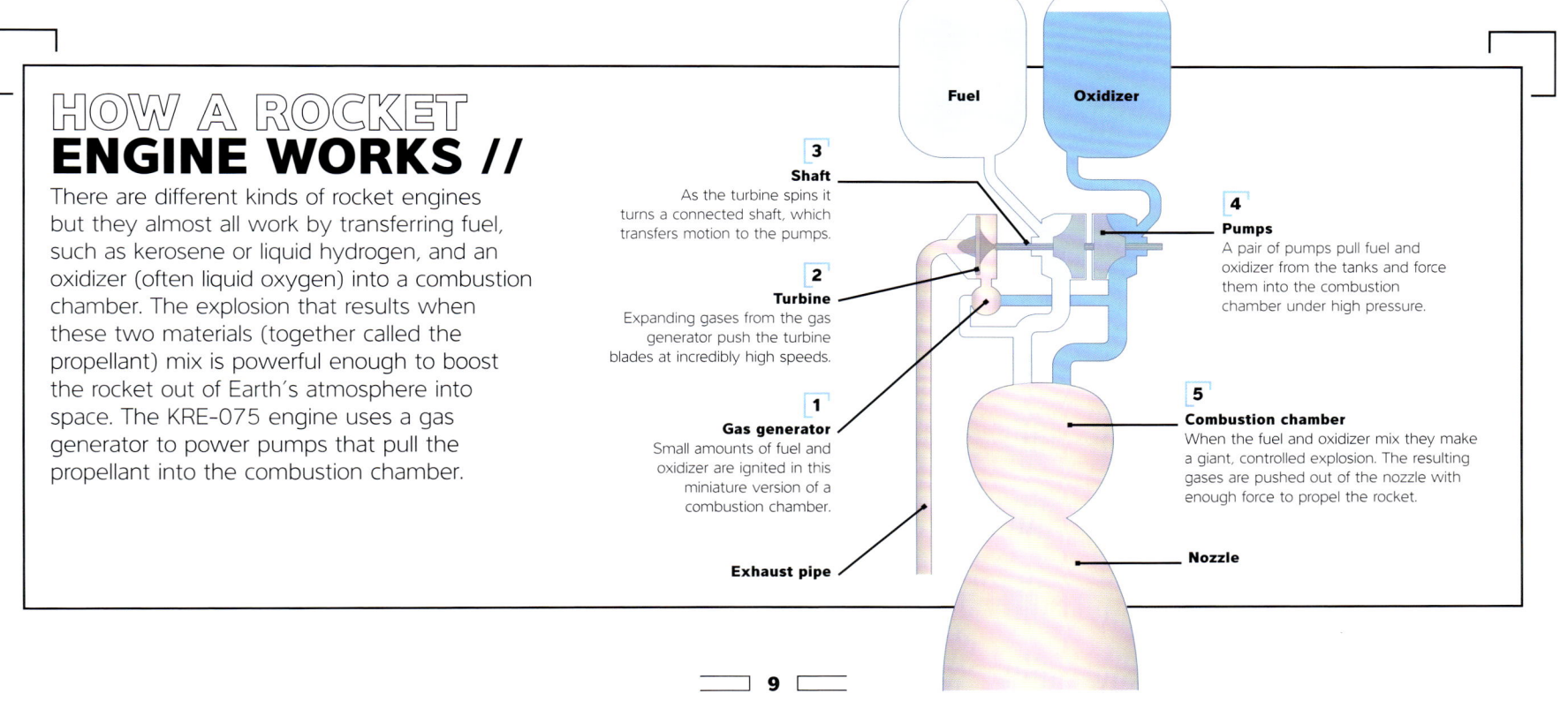

Fuel

Oxidizer

3 Shaft
As the turbine spins it turns a connected shaft, which transfers motion to the pumps.

4 Pumps
A pair of pumps pull fuel and oxidizer from the tanks and force them into the combustion chamber under high pressure.

2 Turbine
Expanding gases from the gas generator push the turbine blades at incredibly high speeds.

1 Gas generator
Small amounts of fuel and oxidizer are ignited in this miniature version of a combustion chamber.

5 Combustion chamber
When the fuel and oxidizer mix they make a giant, controlled explosion. The resulting gases are pushed out of the nozzle with enough force to propel the rocket.

Exhaust pipe

Nozzle

ROCKET FUEL

In almost any rocket launch only a tiny part of the rocket's mass is due to the engines, payload, and rocket structure. The rest, an incredible 90 per cent, is the rocket's fuel. To take off, a rocket needs an enormous amount of fuel, which is mixed with an oxidizer, typically liquid oxygen. There are a range of fuels that can be used, and each creates a different exhaust plume at launch.

ORANGE FLAME //
Refined kerosene and oxygen
This orange flame on SpaceX's Falcon 9 rocket is created through the burning of RP-1, a fuel made from refined kerosene and liquid oxygen. RP-1 is relatively easy to work with because it is liquid at room temperature and has a lower explosion risk.

BLUE FLAME //
Methane and oxygen
Relativity Space's Terran-1 was the first 3D-printed rocket to reach space. It used methalox, a fuel made from liquid methane and liquid oxygen, which produces a blue flame. As both are gases at room temperature, they must be super-cooled to maintain a liquid form.

WHITE FLAME //
Aluminium
The white plumes at the sides of the Atlas V are created by its solid rocket boosters (SRBs), which provide extra thrust during lift-off. The solid fuel contains aluminium, which produces a brilliant white smoke. The rocket's main engine, seen at the centre, uses RP-1.

TRANSPARENT FLAME //
Liquid oxygen and liquid hydrogen
The main engines of this Long March-5 rocket are powered by liquid hydrogen and oxygen. They create a very clean, powerful reaction that produces just water vapour and an almost transparent flame – seen coming from the central nozzle in this image.

SOLID VS LIQUID //

The first rockets were powered by solid fuel, but many modern rockets use liquid fuel. Liquid fuels are more volatile but they're also more versatile. Once ignited, a solid fuel rocket cannot be shut down, whereas a liquid fuel rocket can be adjusted and restarted. Some rockets use liquid fuel in the main engines and have boosters that contain solid fuel. The boosters drop back to Earth after launch and may be reusable.

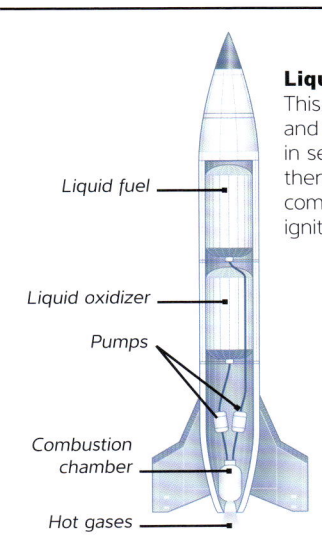

Liquid fuel
This rocket carries liquid fuel and oxidizer (liquid oxygen) in separate tanks. They are then pumped into the combustion chamber and ignited to create thrust.

- Liquid fuel
- Liquid oxidizer
- Pumps
- Combustion chamber
- Hot gases

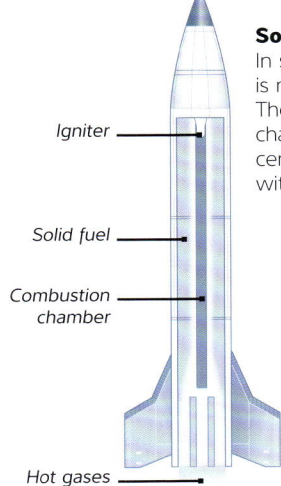

Solid fuel
In solid fuels the oxygen is mixed into the fuel itself. The hollow combustion chamber runs through the centre of the solid fuel, with the igniter at the top.

- Igniter
- Solid fuel
- Combustion chamber
- Hot gases

PEGASUS BARGE //
The enormous core stage of NASA's Space Launch System rolls off the Pegasus barge at the Kennedy Space Center, Florida. It has travelled 1,500 km (900 miles) from Louisiana, along canals, rivers, and over the open ocean. The barge is 100 m (330 ft) long and was built in 1999 to transport the main fuel tanks of the Space Shuttle.

ROCKET TRANSPORTATION

Before a rocket ever gets to the launch pad, it may have travelled great distances over land, air, and sea. The different parts of a rocket are constructed separately in locations that may be very far apart. Once built, these parts must be shipped to the launch site so the rocket can be pieced together. Each step in the journey is carefully planned and monitored to ensure these giant machines get safely to their destination.

WIND POWER //
ESA's Ariane rocket is constructed in Europe then shipped 7,000 km (4,350 miles) across the Atlantic Ocean to its launch site in French Guiana. It travels on a purpose-built barge called *Canopée*. Four huge sails are used alongside the ship's fuel-powered engines.

TAKING THE TRAIN //
Russia's Roscosmos space agency employs a custom railway to get their Soyuz rockets across the deserts of Kazakhstan to the launch pad. It is one of the largest industrial railways in the world and uses specialized freight cars to carry the enormous rockets.

ON THE ROAD //
SpaceX regularly deploys a small fleet of trucks to move its Falcon boosters between their rocket factory and the launch sites. The trucks also recover the boosters after use and take them back to SpaceX facilities. This booster is on its way to make its 22nd flight.

AIR FREIGHT //
Smaller rocket components can be flown via aeroplane. NASA's Super Guppy plane has a very wide cargo bay and a hinged nose that allows the front of the aircraft to open sideways so that large rocket parts and payloads can be stowed.

IN THE LAB //
This image shows one half of the fairing that will form a protective nose cone at the top of the Delta IV Heavy rocket. After the fairing has been constructed, it is moved and placed around the payload in a process called encapsulation.

Lightweight materials
The fairings are made of a carbon composite, which is tough but light so it won't add much extra weight to the rocket.

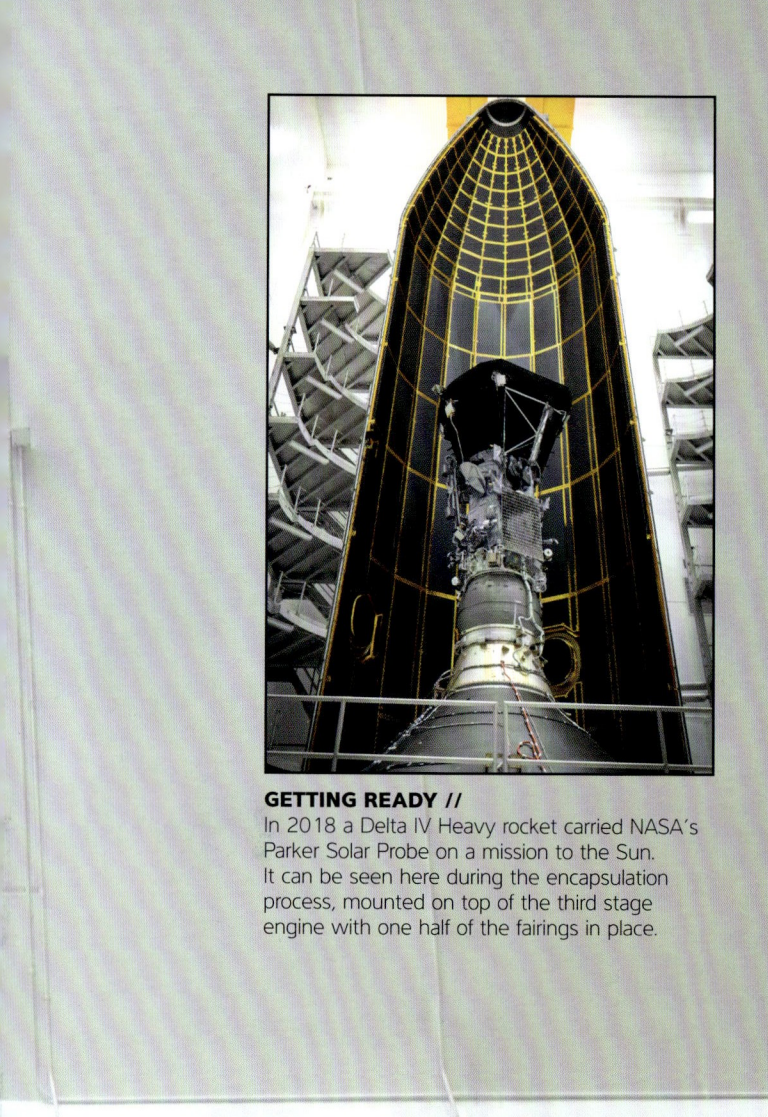

GETTING READY //
In 2018 a Delta IV Heavy rocket carried NASA's Parker Solar Probe on a mission to the Sun. It can be seen here during the encapsulation process, mounted on top of the third stage engine with one half of the fairings in place.

RELEASING THE PAYLOAD //
The fairings are built in two pieces so they can split apart to release the payload. The James Webb Space Telescope is nearly as big as a tennis court, so it had to be folded to fit inside the Ariane 5's fairings. After its launch in December 2021, it took a month to unfold fully.

PROTECTING THE PAYLOAD

The cargo that a rocket carries into space is called its payload and it is mounted at the very top of the rocket. Satellite payloads are shielded from the forces at launch by fairings – an outer shell that detaches when a rocket has reached space. The payload is then released and continues to its final destination.

PAYLOAD CAPACITY //

The amount of load a rocket can carry often depends on its destination. The same rocket would be able to carry a heavier load into low Earth orbit than it would further into space. The biggest rockets can send payloads of more than 20 tonnes (22 tons) into low Earth orbit.

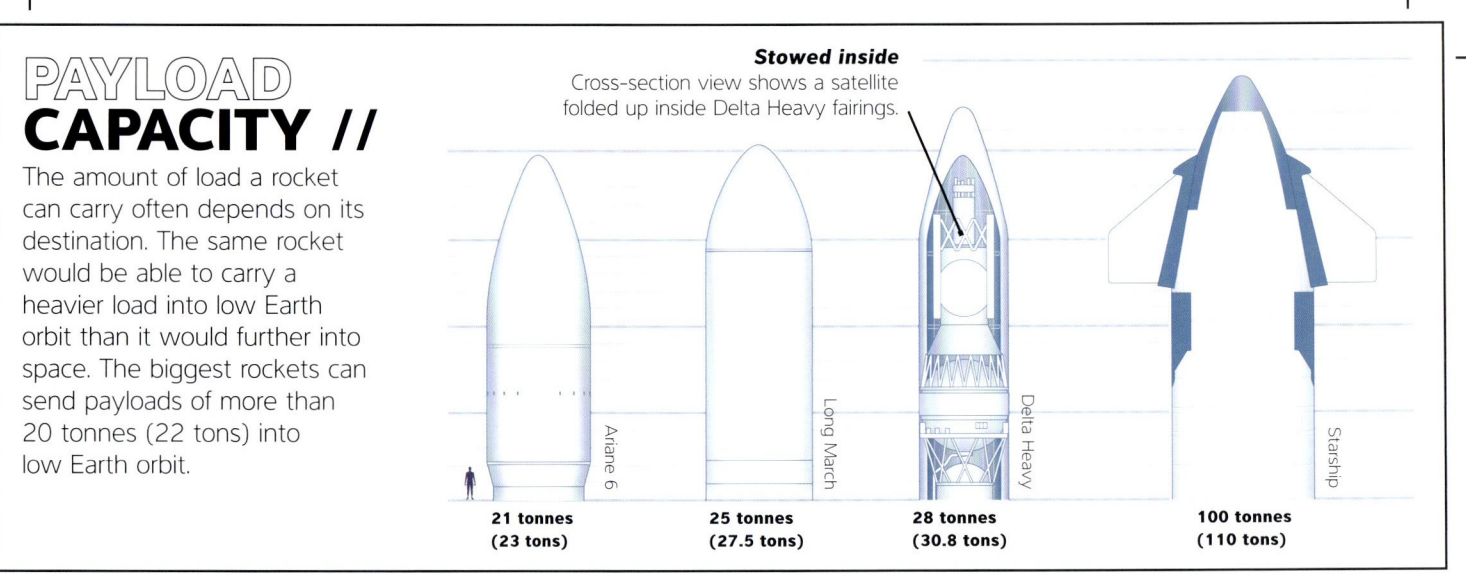

Stowed inside
Cross-section view shows a satellite folded up inside Delta Heavy fairings.

Ariane 6	Long March	Delta Heavy	Starship
21 tonnes (23 tons)	25 tonnes (27.5 tons)	28 tonnes (30.8 tons)	100 tonnes (110 tons)

SUPER STACKING

The different parts of a multi-stage rocket are constructed separately, so almost every rocket goes through a process called stacking to get it ready for lift-off. The sections of the rocket are stacked on top of each other and then firmly attached. Most rockets are stacked vertically, like this Vulcan rocket. However some are stacked horizontally and then raised up so they are pointing at the sky (see page 38).

1 GOING VERTICAL //
The first step is to get the rocket standing up. The Vulcan's first stage is raised by crane, and carefully guided into position within a purpose-built structure called the Vertical Integration Facility (VIF).

2 INSTALLING THE BOOSTERS //
Next the boosters, containing solid fuel, are lifted up and lowered into position. They are strapped to the first stage with bolts that can be ejected when the rocket is in flight and the boosters' fuel has been used up.

3 HOISTING THE UPPER STAGE //
The upper stage of the Vulcan is called Centaur V. It is lifted onto the top of the first stage. Between the two sections is a piece called the interstage – a hollow ring that connects the two parts and protects the upper stage engines during flight.

Payload fairings
The curved top of a rocket is a protective shell. It shields the equipment or capsule while the rocket moves through the atmosphere.

Centaur V
The Vulcan rocket has two main sections, or stages. Once the rocket is above most of Earth's atmosphere, the Centaur V upper stage will fire to propel the payload into orbit.

First stage
The first stage of any rocket is the most powerful. It has to push the rocket through the thick air of the lower atmosphere, which adds resistance that slows the rocket down.

4 FULLY STACKED //
The payload or capsule takes its place at the top of the rocket. When all the pieces are in position, the connections are checked and the rocket is ready to go.

5 READY TO ROLL //
The rocket is stacked directly onto its launch platform, so that it can roll out of the Vertical Integration Facility and begin the slow, careful journey to the launch pad.

Mobile launch platform
The mobile launch platform carries the rocket to the launch pad. It also provides power and communications connections and will support the fuelling process before take-off.

VEHICLE ASSEMBLY BUILDING

To stack the biggest rockets, you need a supersized building. NASA's enormous Vehicle Assembly Building (VAB) provides one of the biggest internal spaces in the world. It was built in 1966 for the Apollo program and used throughout the life of the Space Shuttle. Today it is used to assemble the Space Launch System (SLS) rocket that NASA hopes will soon send humans back to the Moon (see pages 54-55).

Massive Moon rocket
In High Bay 3 the SLS rocket and Orion spacecraft are fully stacked in preparation for the 2022 Artemis I mission to the Moon.

HIGH BAY 3 //
The VAB is the height of a 50-storey building and is split into four high bays, each of which is used to assemble rockets. Work platforms surround the rocket and allow the team access to every element during the precise assembly and testing procedure.

Access platforms
The ten levels of work platforms can slide towards and away from the rocket. Here they are retracted because work on the rocket is complete.

KENNEDY
CENTER //

The Kennedy Space Center has been NASA's primary launch centre since 1968. It contains a wide range of facilities for the launch of space missions. This includes the VAB, Launch Control Center, two launch pads, dormitories and training sites for astronauts, and even a public visitor centre. In recent years Kennedy has been opened to private companies, allowing them to rent the facilities to perform space missions.

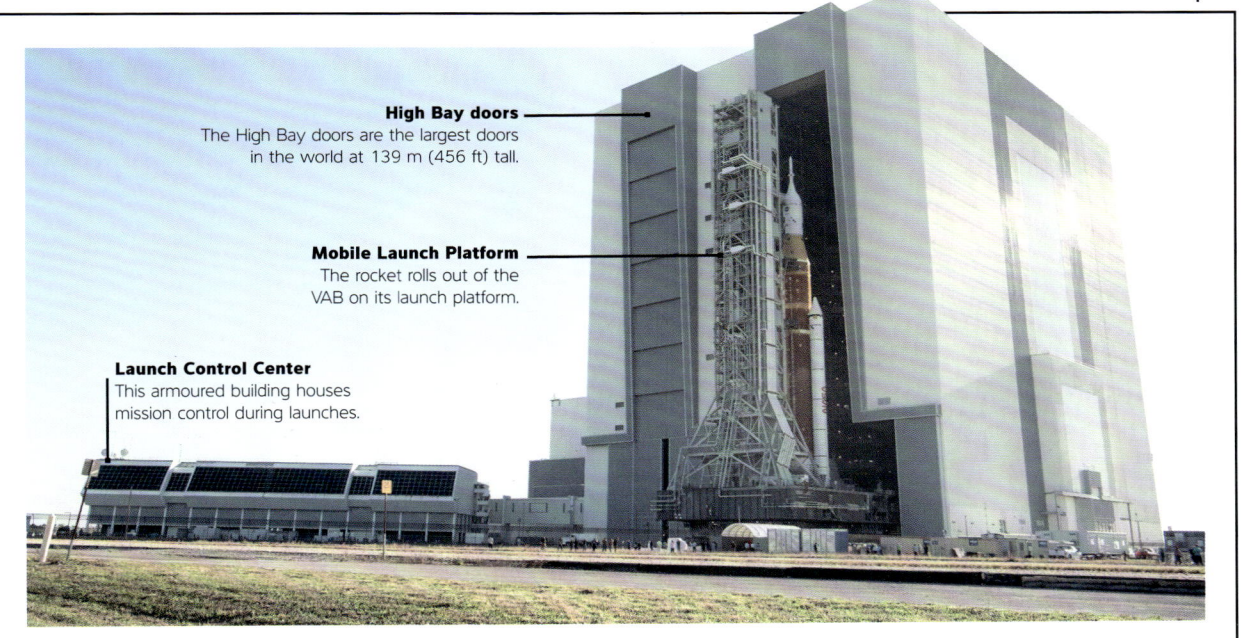

High Bay doors
The High Bay doors are the largest doors in the world at 139 m (456 ft) tall.

Mobile Launch Platform
The rocket rolls out of the VAB on its launch platform.

Launch Control Center
This armoured building houses mission control during launches.

CRAWLER TRANSPORTER //

NASA built two crawler transporters in 1965, to carry rockets such as the Saturn V to the launch pads at the Kennedy Space Center in Florida, USA. The crawlers are the largest and heaviest self-propelled vehicles in the world. They have been used more than 300 times and in recent years have been modified to carry the SLS rocket.

Slow but steady //
Rockets are transported upright on a mobile launcher. The crawler's top speed is just over 1.6 km/h (1 mph).

Crawlerways //
Roads made of rocks support the mammoth crawlers and allow them to turn without damaging their cargo.

Perfect conditions //
The crawlerways are sprayed with water to prevent dust getting caught in the crawler's system.

ROLL TO THE LAUNCH PAD

The final stage of a rocket's journey to the launch pad is one of the most crucial. NASA uses gigantic, tracked vehicles called crawler transporters to carry rockets from the Vehicle Assembly Building (VAB) to the launch sites. The journey is only about 6.4 km (4 miles), but it takes around six hours.

Service tower
The crawler transports the launch tower – a tall, fixed framework that provides fuel and gives astronauts and engineers access to the rocket for servicing and maintenance.

SUPER CRAWLER //
In November 2022, a modified "super crawler" transporter carefully rolled the mighty SLS rocket and Orion spacecraft from the VAB to the launch pad in preparation for the Artemis I mission to the Moon (see pages 54–55). Once in place, the rocket had to be thoroughly checked and tested again before being passed fit for launch.

Heavy load
The super crawler can carry a load of more than 8,200 tonnes (8,820 tons), which is about the equivalent of 20 long-haul, fully loaded passenger planes.

Mobile launch platform
The crawler also carries the mobile launch platform – a structure that supports the SLS on the launch pad.

GO FOR LAUNCH

When the rocket is ready, the final launch sequence starts, using the T-minus countdown. The "T" stands for "time", meaning the time that the rocket is scheduled to launch. The "minus" refers to the hours and minutes being counted down. At T-0, the engines fire, the connectors attaching the rocket to the launch pad release, the arms swing back, and the rocket lifts off.

GO OR NO GO //
India's LVM3 rocket had a 24-hour countdown before lifting off from Satish Dhawan Space Centre in March 2023. In the final hours before launch, the team checks the weather conditions, the rocket is fuelled, and all crew members leave the launch pad. In the last few minutes, the launch director gets confirmation from the crew that all systems are working correctly and says "go for launch".

Access all areas
Platforms at various levels on the mobile launcher are used to access, test, and check different parts of the rocket before launch.

WATER DELUGE //
The vibrations generated when a rocket launches can damage the surrounding area and the rocket itself. Spraying water during launch helps to reduce the vibrations and creates an impressive cloud of water vapour (steam). Above, engineers at SpaceX test their water deluge system ahead of their next launch.

UMBILICAL CONNECTIONS //
Before lift-off, the rocket is connected to the mobile launcher via connectors known as umbilicals. Pictured here on the Ariane 5, different lines supply power, coolant, and fuel, and enable communications. The sturdy outer arms support the rocket and keep it steady.

FILLING THE FUEL TANKS //
Some liquid fuels (see page 10) present extra challenges because they have to be kept super cool in special tanks before being transferred carefully to the rocket just before launch. Some of the fuel boils off before launch and is vented, creating clouds of gas, as seen on this Falcon 9 rocket on the launch pad.

LAUNCH CONTROL CENTRE //
The countdown to launch can start as much as 72 hours before lift-off and everything is coordinated, to the second, by the people in the control centre. Here, a NASA team are preparing to launch the James Webb Telescope aboard the Ariane 5 rocket on Christmas Day 2021.

BLAST OFF!

As the engines roar into life, a rocket's fuel is ignited and gas and flames are directed out through the engine nozzles. Millions of newtons of force start to lift the rocket and its cargo off the ground. A rocket launch is really a colossal controlled explosion, so this is a nerve-wracking moment for mission teams. Any small error could have disastrous results.

ATLAS V //
An Atlas V rocket blasts off from Cape Canaveral, USA, in 2012, carrying a US Navy satellite. This rocket has two main stages and up to five solid rocket boosters, and is operated by US company United Launch Alliance. Atlas V rockets have taken off more than 100 times, with a near-perfect success rate.

Fiery plume
The solid fuel from the strap-on boosters burns brightly with a yellow flame.

Billowing clouds
A huge cloud of smoke and steam engulfs the launch pad.

ACTION AND REACTION //

The forces that govern a rocket launch were first explained by English scientist Isaac Newton in 1687, in his *Laws of Motion*. Newton's third law states that for every action there is an equal and opposite reaction. This means that when one object exerts a force on another object, the second object pushes back on the first object with equal force. In a rocket launch, the force of gas and flames pushing their way out of the engines creates an opposite reaction force, providing the lift the rocket needs to take off.

Rocket at rest
Unless a force acts on the rocket, it won't move.

Lift-off
The hot gases push downwards at high speed. The rocket is pushed upwards with equal force.

On the launch pad
Before launch, forces are balanced. Gravity pulls on the rocket, but Earth's surface pushes up with equal force.

Ignition
The engines fire and create a force by pushing out hot gas and flames. A reaction force acts on the rocket in the opposite direction.

Lift-off
As long as the force created by the engines is greater than the force of gravity the rocket will accelerate and rise into the air.

GUIDANCE SYSTEMS

Modern rockets have very high-tech guidance systems to keep them stable in flight and to control their direction. This is because lots of different forces are acting on a rocket in flight, and it is also moving incredibly fast. Without these internal guidance systems, the rocket would wobble, veer off course, and be more likely to fail in its mission, or even crash.

Second stage
This section of the rocket holds the guidance system, which contains sensors, computers, and radars.

LE-5A engine
The H-IIA rocket's engines constantly make small adjustments to the left and to the right to keep the rocket moving in a straight line (see panel below).

STAYING ON COURSE //
Here, Japan's H-IIA-37 rocket lifts off from the launch pad at Tanegashima Space Centre in 2017 on a mission to put two satellites into different orbits for the first time. Internal sensors measure the rocket's position very accurately, and then the rocket's navigation system uses this information to adjust the direction of the rocket's thrust automatically, which in turn alters the rocket's direction.

ENGINE
GIMBALLING //

A rocket's engines are not fixed in one position but are mounted on devices called gimbals, which allow the engines to move and change the rocket's direction. Commonly known as gimballing, this change in direction happens automatically and very quickly via lots of tiny movements. Engine gimballing is especially useful in modern, reusable rockets that need precise navigation when landing back on the launch pad.

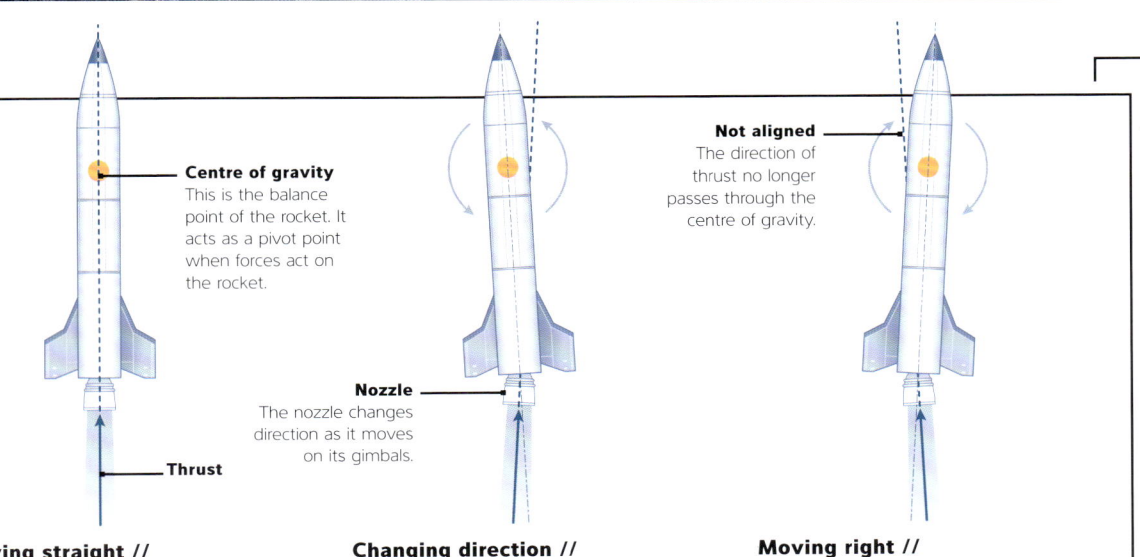

Centre of gravity
This is the balance point of the rocket. It acts as a pivot point when forces act on the rocket.

Nozzle
The nozzle changes direction as it moves on its gimbals.

Not aligned
The direction of thrust no longer passes through the centre of gravity.

Thrust

Staying straight //
When the engine nozzle is straight, the direction of thrust is aligned with the rocket's centre of gravity. The rocket travels in a straight line.

Changing direction //
When the engine nozzle swings a little to the left, the direction of thrust is no longer aligned with the centre of gravity. This causes a force that makes the rocket nose veer left.

Moving right //
When the engine nozzle swings to the right, the force produced makes the rocket nose turn to the right. Making lots of small corrections keeps the rocket on course.

HEAT TRAIL

Like a ship moving through the sea, a rocket leaves behind a trail in its wake. The rocket's engines burn colossal amounts of fuel, creating exhaust gases that show the rocket's journey through the atmosphere. As launches become more and more frequent, the trails they leave behind during take-off are becoming a familiar sight for people living close to launch sites.

Satellite payload
This launch placed two Intelsat communications satellites into geostationary orbit. They will be used to broadcast television services across North America.

Exhaust plume
The exhaust gases from the rocket's Merlin engines are incredibly hot – more than 1,000°C (1,800°F).

TWILIGHT PHENOMENA //

Near launch sites, there has been a rise in the sightings of a mysterious "space jellyfish". This is not a cosmic sea creature but in fact the plume of a passing rocket. As the rocket gets higher, the air becomes thinner and the trail starts to spread out. This creates an eerie expanding cloud that lingers after the rocket has gone, catching the light at dawn or dusk.

The launch of a Soyuz rocket creates a space jellyfish effect

A Falcon 9 launch seen over Phoenix, Arizona

Vapour trail
The hot gases disrupt the surrounding air, causing water vapour in and around the exhaust plume to condense and create a cloudy trail.

SHIMMERING TRAIL //
A SpaceX Falcon 9 rocket launches in October 2022, against the backdrop of the full Moon. The Falcon 9 first stage engines burn a mixture of kerosene and liquid oxygen, creating a bright yellow-white plume. The hot gases interact with the gases in the atmosphere, leaving a visible trail even after the rocket has passed.

VAPOUR TRAIL //
United Launch Alliance's Atlas V rocket launched in September 2023, leaving behind a stunning smoky plume, which shows its tilted flight path. It is carrying a satellite into an orbit 35,000 km (22,000 miles) above Earth.

Moving sideways
The rocket travels fast while gravity pulls down on it, sending the rocket on a curved flight path.

FLIGHT PATH

Regardless of their ultimate destination, all rockets begin their mission travelling the same way – vertically. At lift-off they use enormous amounts of thrust to get clear of the launch pad. Then, any rockets that are heading into orbit must tilt sideways in what is known as a "gravity turn". This manoeuvre uses Earth's gravity to pull the rocket onto a curved path.

Vertical launch
The very start of a rocket's journey is vertical, taking off at a 90° angle before it starts to lean over and convert its speed into sideways motion.

GRAVITY TURN //

To stay in space, a rocket must reach orbit – a position where it is travelling forwards so quickly that its speed balances the pull of Earth's gravity so that it travels in a curved path around the planet. Rockets follow a curved launch path because the quicker the rocket can curve over, the quicker it can start building up enough sideways speed to achieve orbit.

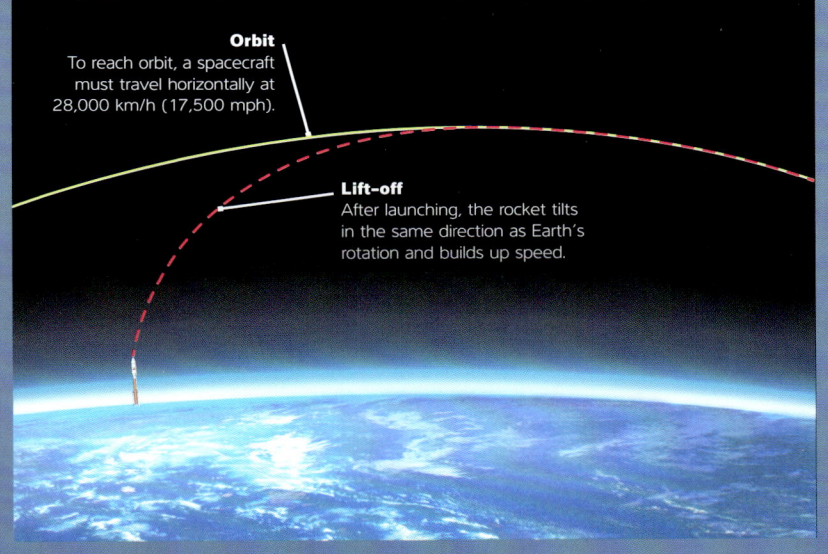

Orbit
To reach orbit, a spacecraft must travel horizontally at 28,000 km/h (17,500 mph).

Lift-off
After launching, the rocket tilts in the same direction as Earth's rotation and builds up speed.

"ESA'S ARIANE

The European Space Agency (ESA) specializes in launching large satellites for space exploration. To do this, they use the Ariane family of launchers. First flown in 1996, Ariane 5 was ESA's heavy-lift rocket for many years. Now Ariane 6 is set to take over as Europe's new launch system.

FIRST FLIGHT OF ARIANE 6 //
In July 2024, Ariane 6 blasted off for the first time from Europe's Spaceport in French Guiana, releasing its satellite payload 600 km (370 miles) above Earth. The launch was successful but not perfect. The final step of the mission was meant to send the upper stage back down to Earth, leaving no space debris behind, but a small fault meant the upper stage engines failed to fire.

Mechanical arms
Before launch, two "cryo-arms" supply the super-cooled fuel to the main tank. The arms swing back as the rocket lifts off.

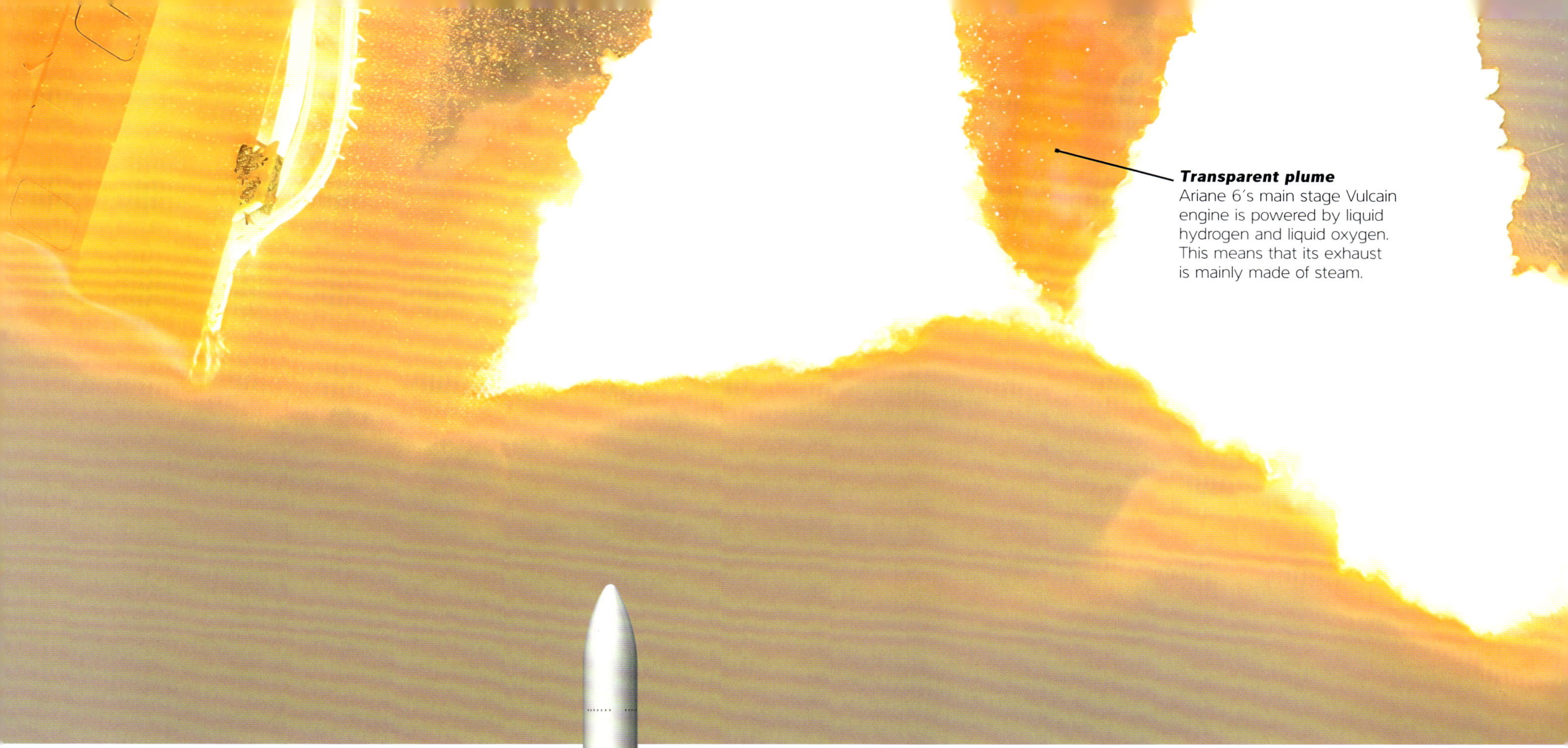

Transparent plume
Ariane 6's main stage Vulcain engine is powered by liquid hydrogen and liquid oxygen. This means that its exhaust is mainly made of steam.

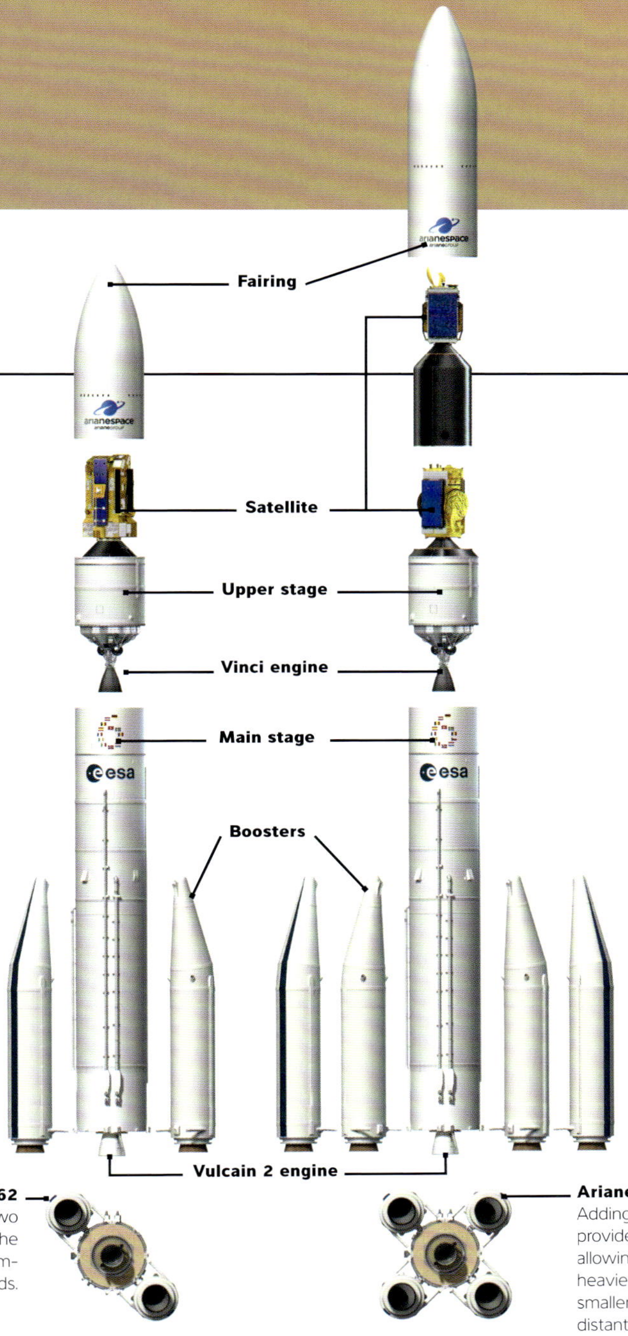

- Fairing
- Satellite
- Upper stage
- Vinci engine
- Main stage
- Boosters
- Vulcan 2 engine

Ariane 62
Attaching two boosters allows the rocket to lift medium-sized payloads.

Ariane 64
Adding four boosters provides extra thrust, allowing the rocket to lift heavier payloads or carry smaller ones to more distant orbits.

ARIANE 6 //

The Ariane 6's main engine is an improvement on its predecessor, being easier and cheaper to build while still delivering the same power. This combines with a brand-new engine for the second stage, designed to ensure the best performance for launching new satellites. The rocket can be configured with either two or four boosters depending on the mission it is undertaking.

ARIANE 5 //

In service for 27 years, Ariane 5 successfully flew more than 100 times, launching several landmark space missions. It launched the Rosetta spacecraft in 2004, which was the first mission ever to land a probe on a comet. In 2021 it launched the James Webb Space Telescope into orbit 1.5 million km (930,000 miles) from Earth. One of its final flights in 2023 sent the JUICE mission on its way to explore the moons of Jupiter.

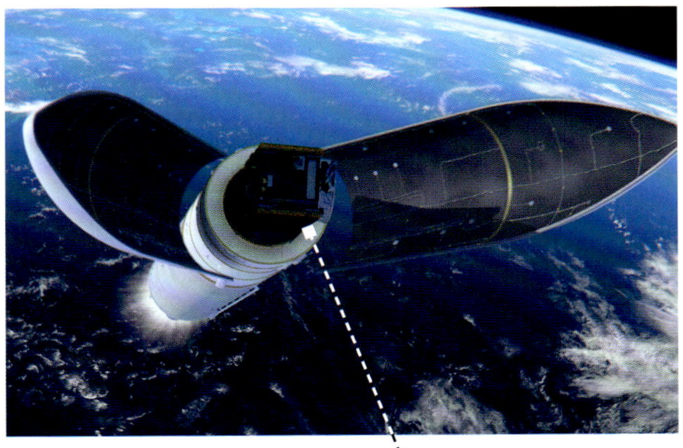

Ariane 5 launches JUICE
In this artist's impression, Ariane 5 is seen releasing the JUICE spacecraft half an hour after lift-off. The spacecraft will take eight years to reach Jupiter.

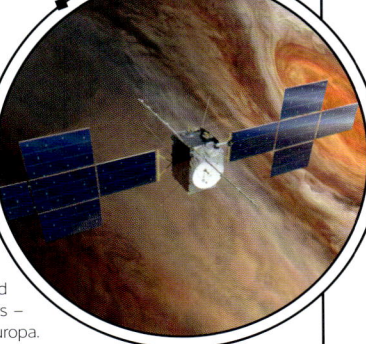

Destination Jupiter
Due to arrive in 2031, JUICE will orbit the giant planet and study three of its largest moons – Ganymede, Callisto, and Europa.

STAGE SEPARATION

When Ariane 6 made its first flight in July 2024, the launch was filmed by cameras mounted on the rocket itself. The pictures give a clear view of the process known as stage separation or staging, where parts of the rocket no longer needed are jettisoned and fall back to Earth.

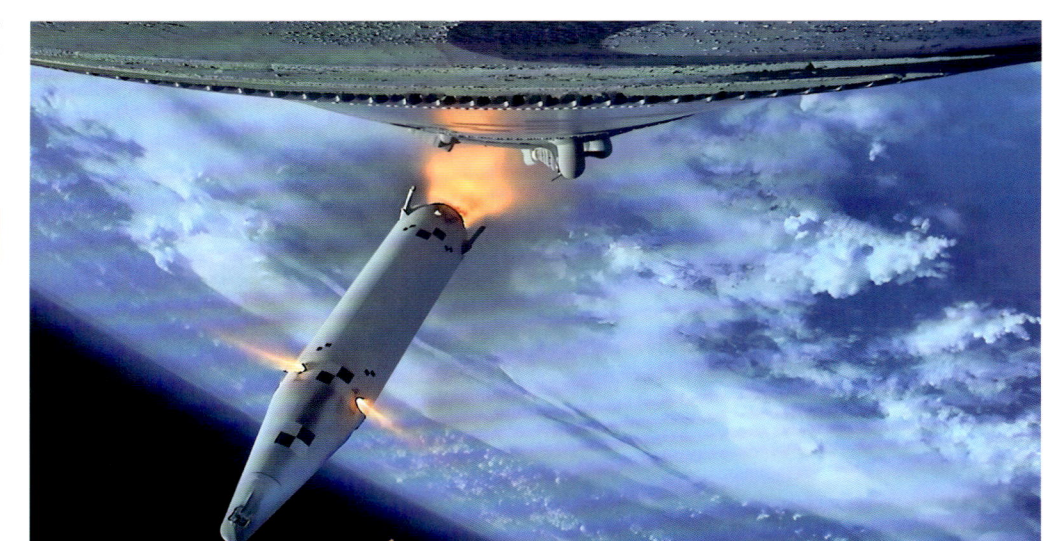

1

WE HAVE LIFT-OFF! //
The rocket powers upwards, propelled by the main stage engines and the solid rocket boosters strapped to its sides. Just two minutes after launch, the rocket has left the thickest layers of Earth's atmosphere behind and burned more than 280 tonnes (308 tons) of fuel.

Solid rocket booster
This view of the booster is captured from above, by a camera attached to the side of the rocket.

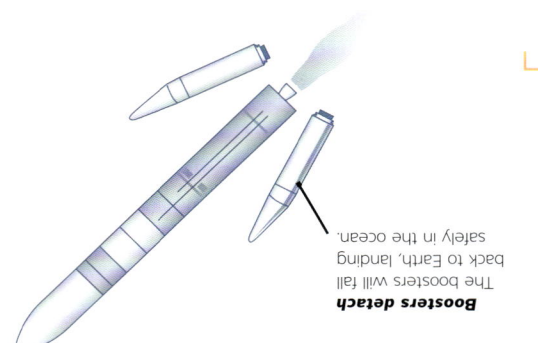

2

BOOSTER SEPARATION //
Less than two and a half minutes after launch, the fuel in the solid rocket boosters is spent and they need to be jettisoned. Explosive bolts fire to detach each booster from the main stage. Then small separation rockets at the top of the booster fire, to push it safely away from the main stage, preventing a collision.

Boosters detach
The boosters will fall back to Earth, landing safely in the ocean.

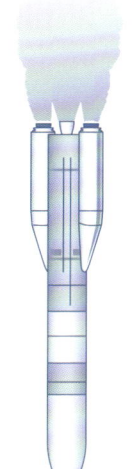

STAGING SEQUENCE //

Each step in the staging process must happen smoothly for a successful launch. The steps are programmed to happen automatically rather than being controlled from Earth. This sequence shows the staging process for Ariane 6. Each numbered step is pictured below.

CubeSat
On this mission Ariane 6 was carrying CubeSats on behalf of various space agencies, private companies, and universities.

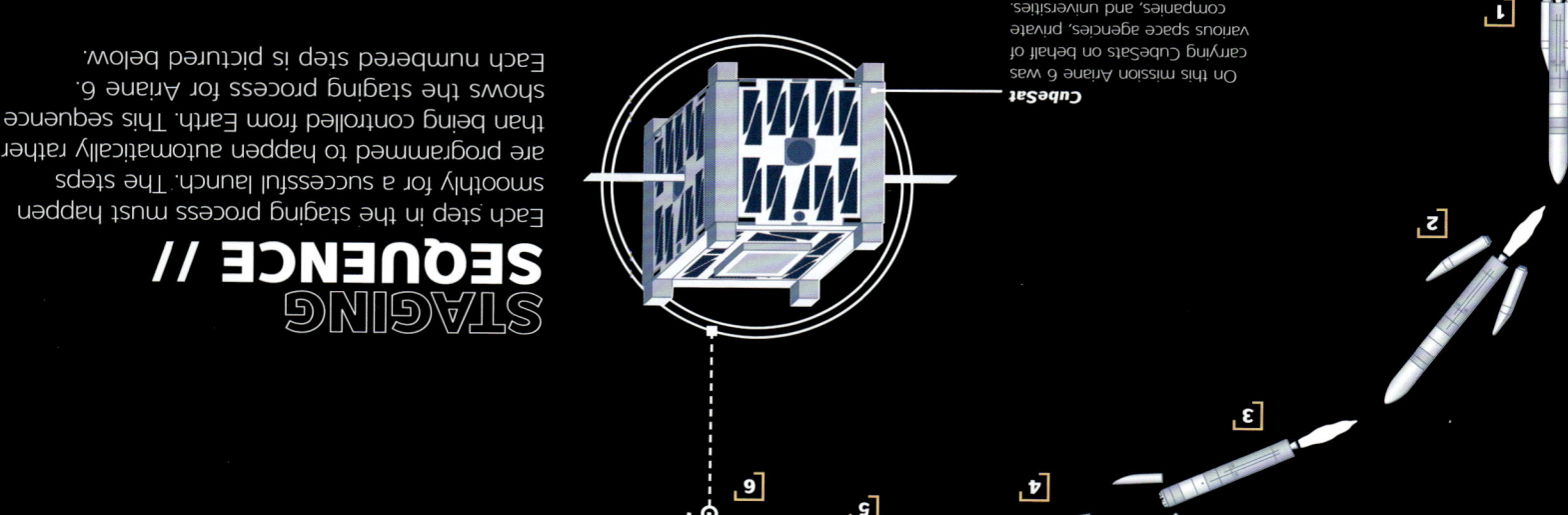

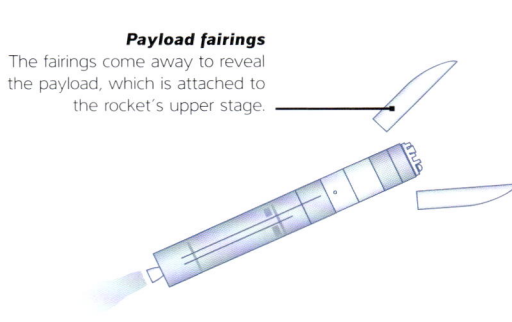

Payload fairings
The fairings come away to reveal the payload, which is attached to the rocket's upper stage.

3

FAIRINGS JETTISONED //
Next, the fairings protecting the payload come away. Two fairings form the nose cone on the top of the rocket. Three minutes into the launch, the fairings break away from the rocket and fall back to Earth.

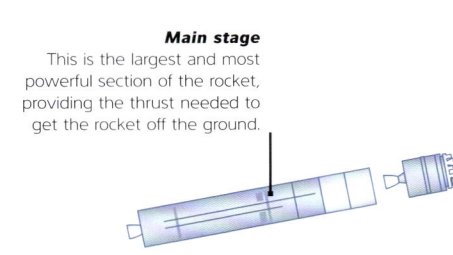

Main stage
This is the largest and most powerful section of the rocket, providing the thrust needed to get the rocket off the ground.

4

MAIN STAGE SEPARATES //
Just under eight minutes after launch the fuel in the main stage is used up. The bolts attaching the main stage to the rest of the rocket are released, and it falls back towards Earth, splashing down in the Pacific Ocean.

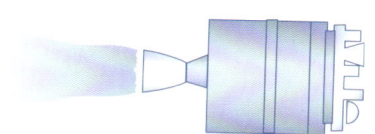

5

UPPER STAGE ENGINE FIRES //
The upper stage then pushes the payload into orbit 580 km (360 miles) above Earth. The craft is now travelling in a curved path around Earth. This view is from a camera inside the rocket's upper stage. The red glow is the upper stage engine.

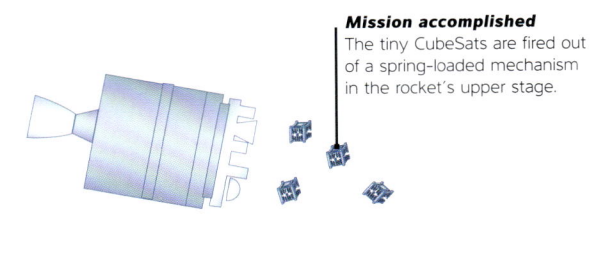

Mission accomplished
The tiny CubeSats are fired out of a spring-loaded mechanism in the rocket's upper stage.

6

PAYLOAD RELEASED //
When the upper stage reaches the correct location, the satellite payload is released. In this image, a CubeSat is being ejected into orbit. On this flight, Ariane 6 was carrying a packed payload of eight different satellite missions.

SPACEX STARSHIP

The Starship is the biggest, most powerful rocket ever built. Developed by US company SpaceX, it is still in its testing phase but it is intended to power the next generation of space exploration, reaching the Moon and even Mars. At 123 m (403 ft) tall, Starship is made up of two stages – the Super Heavy booster and the Starship spacecraft.

Starship spacecraft
The second stage has a payload capacity of more than 100 tonnes (110 tons). It will carry both crew and cargo.

Super Heavy booster
The first stage of Starship uses around 3,400 tonnes (3,750 tons) of propellant to lift the rocket off the ground.

ROBOTIC ARMS //

The Starship rocket is intended to be fully reusable. After launch, both the booster and spacecraft will come apart during the mission and land back at the launch site separately. The booster will arrive first and be caught by a pair of robotic arms called the "chopsticks". The spacecraft will follow soon after. The rocket can then be serviced and refuelled, ready to launch again.

- **Launch mount** — A raised platform holds Starship off the ground to prevent damage.
- **Super Heavy booster**
- **Stabilizer arm**
- **Starship spacecraft**
- **Chopsticks** — Two mechanical arms hold the rocket in place before launch.

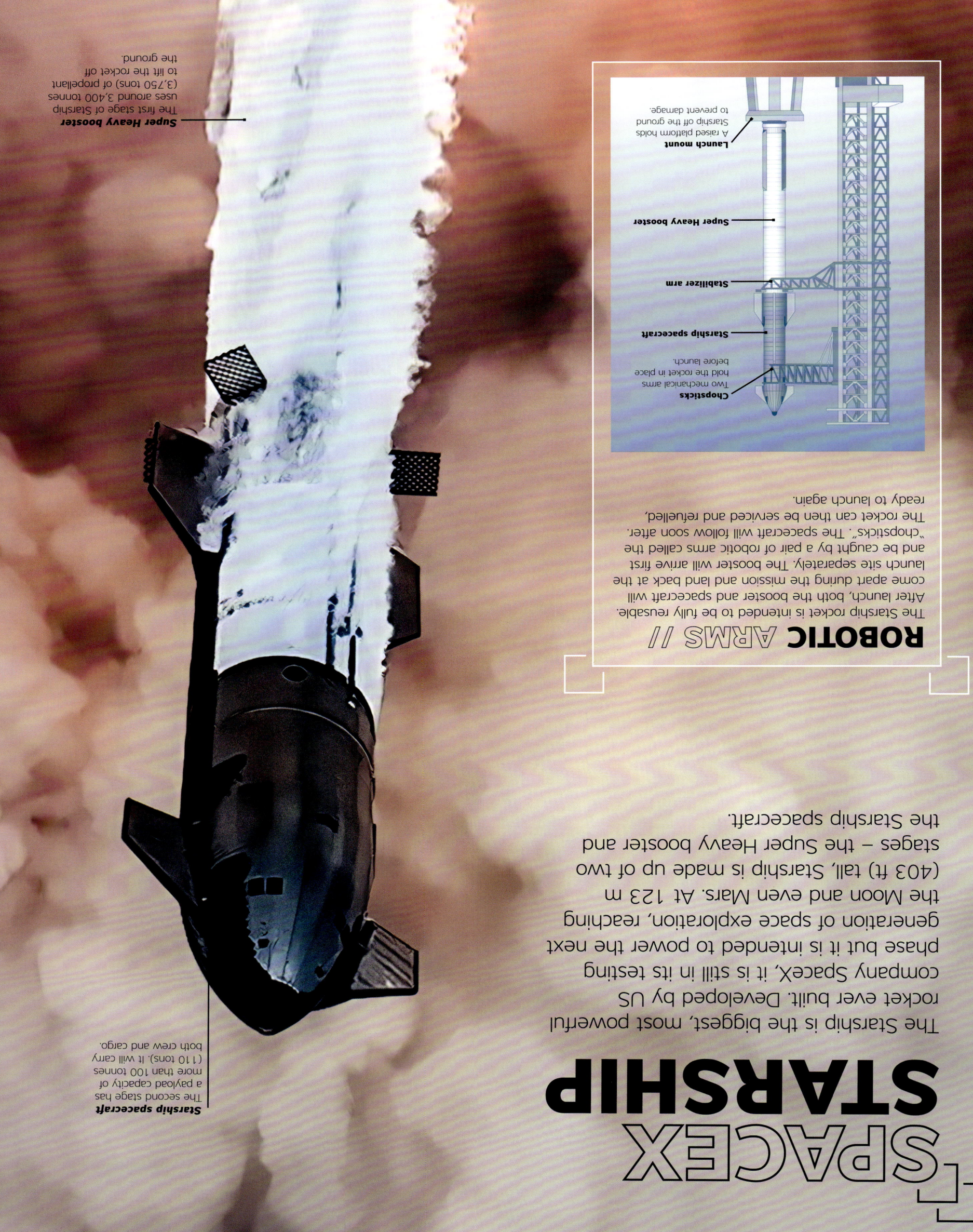

Mechanical arms
The arms move out of the way when Starship launches and swing back together to catch the spacecraft when it returns.

TEST FLIGHT //
SpaceX is still in the early stages of testing Starship to better understand how the rocket performs. Shown here is the launch of flight test four in June 2024. Eventually SpaceX intends to land the booster and the spacecraft but on this test flight both stages splashed down in the ocean as planned.

SUPER SIZE //
At a massive 10 m (32 ft) wide, Starship dwarfs the engineers stacking the spacecraft on top of the Super Heavy booster in August 2021. The booster has 33 Raptor engines powered by liquid methane and liquid oxygen, while the spacecraft has six.

MISSION TO MARS //
Starship has been designed to be powerful enough to carry equipment and up to 100 people to Mars. For SpaceX, the end goal is to create a permanent city on this red, dusty planet, although so far only robotic craft such as NASA's Curiosity rover (above) have been there.

REUSABLE ROCKETS

Before NASA's Space Shuttle, all rockets could only be used once, meaning they were expendable. Even today, most rockets are single use. Costing millions to build, they simply fall into the ocean after doing their job. However, space agencies and private companies such as SpaceX hope to make it cheaper and quicker to get into space by creating rockets that can be relaunched within hours.

Engines fire
The Super Heavy booster has detached from the Starship upper stage, and is heading back to Earth. Thirteen of its 33 Raptor engines are firing to steer it back to the launch site.

SUCCESSFUL CATCH //
Super Heavy is the first stage of SpaceX's Starship rocket. This enormous booster is designed to launch the huge spacecraft (also called Starship) and then separate and return to the launch pad so it can be used again. During its fifth test flight, in October 2024, the returning booster was caught for the first time, seen here in a time-lapse image.

Steering control
Four steel grid fins at the top of the rocket help guide the booster back to Earth.

Coming in hot!
On this flight a fire broke out but it did not prevent a successful catch. Test flights are designed to check performance and fix problems like this.

OTHER
REUSABLES //

Many organizations are developing reusable rockets, which will make getting to space cheaper and quicker. SpaceX's ambitious aim is to make the Falcon Heavy rocket ready for relaunch within 60 minutes. The reusable rockets below both feature special "legs", designed to stabilize them as they land back on Earth.

ZHUQUE-3 //
This stainless steel rocket is being developed in China. Its reusable first stage is powered by nine engines. Zhuque-3 is still in the testing phase and is just one of several reusable rockets being developed in China.

FALCON 9 //
With more than 500 missions completed already, SpaceX's Falcon 9 is leading the way for reusable rockets. Paired with a Dragon spacecraft, it has made more than 20 trips to the ISS. It lands on a floating ocean barge, unfurling four landing legs.

That's a catch
Less than five minutes after launch, the Super Heavy is caught by the launch pad's arms, nicknamed "mechazilla".

1 LIFT TO VERTICAL //
The Soyuz is assembled horizontally and then rolled out by train to the launch pad. When it arrives, it is lifted by a huge metal arm to stand vertically.

2 SECURING THE LOAD //
Once the rocket is vertical, four small support arms close in around its waist, holding it in place above a large, deep trench. At launch, the trench will direct the rocket's exhaust gases safely away from the pad.

3 FUELLING UP //
A few hours before lift-off, the rocket is fuelled using liquid oxygen and kerosene. The liquid oxygen creates clouds of steam as it warms to the surrounding temperature.

4 FINAL CHECKS //
Four large gantry arms are then raised to surround the rocket. This forms a structure that allows the launch team to access and check different parts of the Soyuz before the launch.

Launch shroud
The top part of the Soyuz rocket contains the Soyuz capsule, which can hold up to three astronauts. At launch it is covered by a protective shroud.

Boosters
Four strap-on boosters containing fuel produce a surge of power to propel the rocket upwards.

Launch clamps
When the rocket has enough thrust to get off the ground, the launch clamps open up and release it.

5 LIFT-OFF //
At launch, the Soyuz rocket travels 1,640 km (1,020 miles) in less than 10 minutes. Its speed increases by around 50 km/h (30 mph) every second for about nine minutes!

SOYUZ SYSTEM

Developed in Russia in the 1960s, the Soyuz rocket has been in use longer than any other. It is also the most-launched rocket, taking off more than 1,680 times. Used to carry astronauts to and from the International Space Station, the system is made up of two parts – the Soyuz rocket and the Soyuz capsule that holds the crew.

HEADING **HOME** //
This Soyuz capsule is shown leaving the International Space Station (ISS) and returning to Kazakhstan, where it launched six months earlier. Russian cosmonauts use the ISS alongside astronauts from other countries, but Russia is currently planning to build its own space station.

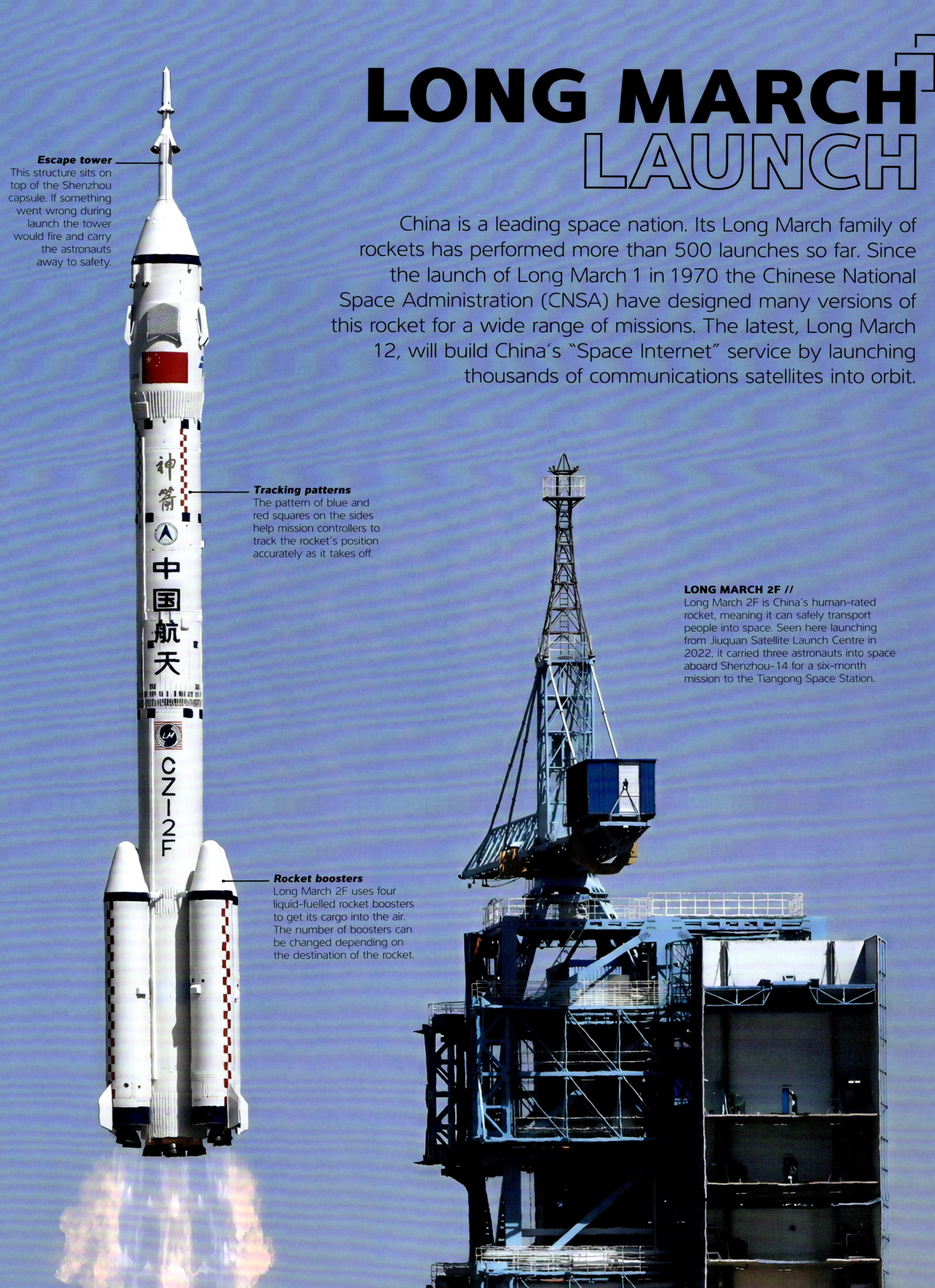

LONG MARCH LAUNCH

China is a leading space nation. Its Long March family of rockets has performed more than 500 launches so far. Since the launch of Long March 1 in 1970 the Chinese National Space Administration (CNSA) have designed many versions of this rocket for a wide range of missions. The latest, Long March 12, will build China's "Space Internet" service by launching thousands of communications satellites into orbit.

Escape tower
This structure sits on top of the Shenzhou capsule. If something went wrong during launch the tower would fire and carry the astronauts away to safety.

Tracking patterns
The pattern of blue and red squares on the sides help mission controllers to track the rocket's position accurately as it takes off.

Rocket boosters
Long March 2F uses four liquid-fuelled rocket boosters to get its cargo into the air. The number of boosters can be changed depending on the destination of the rocket.

LONG MARCH 2F //
Long March 2F is China's human-rated rocket, meaning it can safely transport people into space. Seen here launching from Jiuquan Satellite Launch Centre in 2022, it carried three astronauts into space aboard Shenzhou-14 for a six-month mission to the Tiangong Space Station.

SPACE
NATION //

China's space programme has grown rapidly over the last 50 years to become one of the most capable in the world. China's space agency CNSA operates one of the world's only two space stations. In the next few years it hopes to land astronauts on the Moon and aims to be one of the first agencies to bring rocks back to Earth from the surface of Mars.

Tiangong Space Station //
China's Tiangong Space Station has been in orbit since 2021. So far 23 Chinese astronauts have served missions there. Shown here is the crew of Shenzhou-13.

Shenzhou spacecraft //
The Shenzhou spacecraft (meaning "Divine Vessel") was first flown in November 1999. It has launched 20 times in total, sending China's first astronaut into space in 2003.

SMALL LAUNCHERS

Not every space launch needs a huge, powerful rocket like the SLS or Falcon 9. Sometimes a small-lift launch vehicle (SLLV) will get the job done. This type of rocket can carry payloads of up to 2 tonnes (2.2 tons), and is quicker to build and easier to prepare for launch. Small-lift launch vehicles are ideal for transporting small satellites to low Earth orbit.

STANDING TALL //

It might be called "small", but the Electron is 18 m (59 ft) tall, which is about the same as three adult giraffes standing on top of each other. However, when compared to medium-lift launch vehicles, such as Soyuz, or heavy-lift such as the Falcon Heavy, it does look tiny.

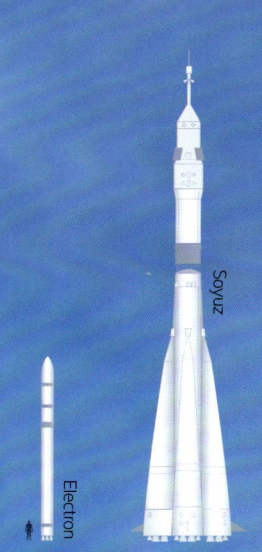

Electron
18 m (59 ft)
Payload capacity to low Earth orbit: 300 kg (660 lb)

Soyuz
49.5 m (162 ft)
Payload capacity to low Earth orbit: around 6,860 kg (15,120 lb)

Falcon Heavy
70 m (230 ft)
Payload capacity to low Earth orbit: 63,800 kg (140,660 lb)

Delivering the payload
The rocket's nose cone protects the payload – here 13 tiny NASA satellites with different functions, including measuring radiation levels and testing 3D robotic arms.

Glittering cloud
As the rocket's fuel is stored at very cold temperatures, ice builds up on the side of the rocket, flaking off as it launches.

ROCKET LAB ELECTRON //
Satellites often hitch a ride on a bigger rocket, where they are not the most important payload on board. However, small-lift launch vehicles can take them to exactly where they need to go. In 2018, this Rocket Lab Electron SLLV blasted off from the Māhia Peninsula in New Zealand carrying miniature satellites known as CubeSats.

CUBESATS //

CubeSats are tiny satellites, which fit in the palm of a hand. A single CubeSat unit (1U) measures 10 cm x 10 cm x 10 cm (4 in x 4 in x 4 in), but CubeSats can be assembled from different numbers of units. They are used for small-scale scientific research, data gathering, and communications.

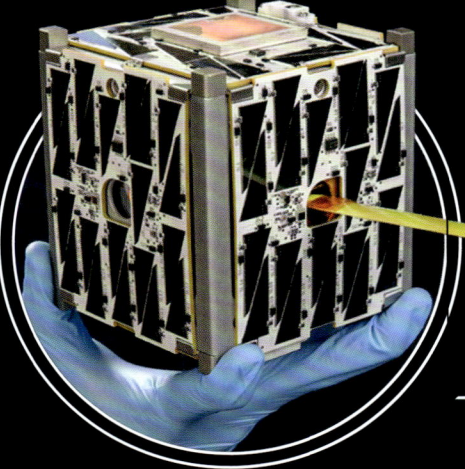

Radio antenna
Most CubeSats have a thin metal antenna to receive and send radio signals.

Size matters
These small satellites cost a lot less to build and launch than traditional satellites, and have much less mass. The most common size of a CubeSat is between 2 and 16 units, which gives them a maximum mass of around 32 kg (70 lb).

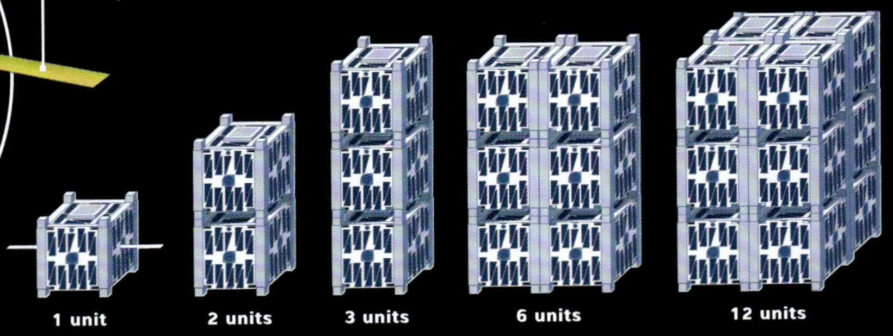

 1 unit

 2 units

 3 units

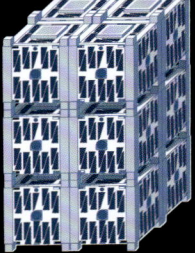 6 units

 12 units

SATELLITE ORBITS

The vast majority of rocket launches are missions to put satellites in orbit. We rely on satellites for internet communication, television and radio broadcasting, navigation systems, and for monitoring the Earth and its neighbourhood in space. Today there are more satellites in orbit around our planet than ever before, with well over 1,000 new satellites launched every year.

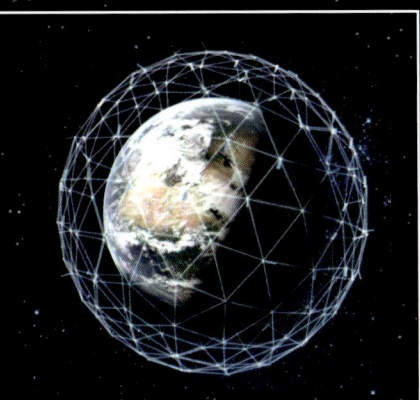

Satellite constellations //
A collection of satellites all working together is called a constellation. These can have hundreds or thousands of satellites. A network like this ensures global coverage, for example for satellite navigation systems.

SMILE
The SMILE satellite monitors the Sun's effect on Earth. It has a highly elliptical orbit, which means part of its orbit is close to Earth and part is a long distance away.

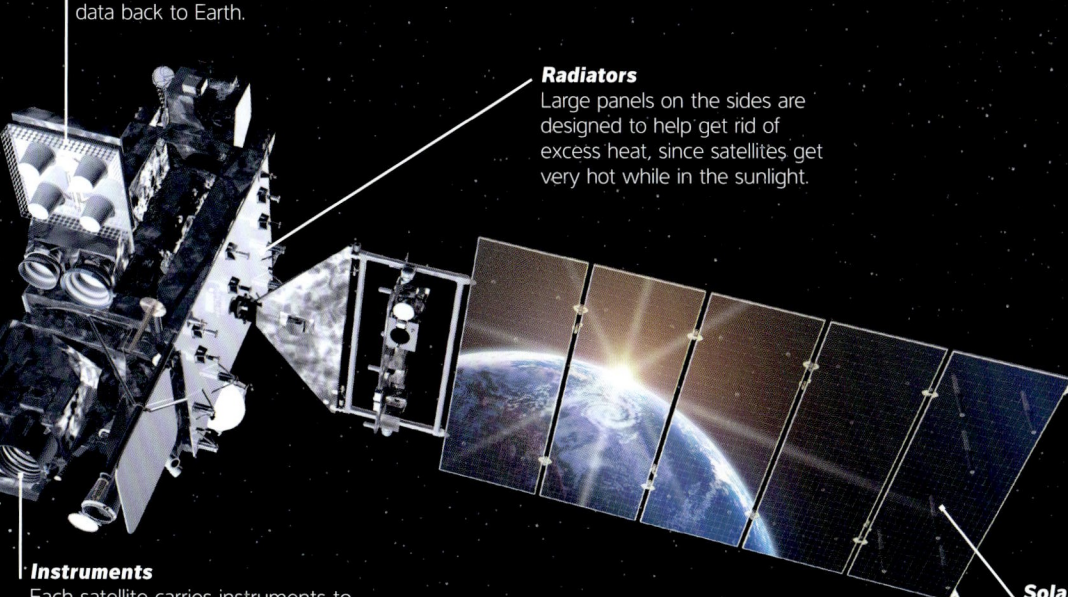

Antenna
The antennas allow the satellite to receive instructions and send data back to Earth.

Radiators
Large panels on the sides are designed to help get rid of excess heat, since satellites get very hot while in the sunlight.

Instruments
Each satellite carries instruments to do a specific job. This satellite has cameras and sensors to monitor the weather.

Solar arrays
Solar panels convert sunlight energy into electricity, and are often used to power satellites. The more power a spacecraft needs, the more solar panels it will have in its arrays.

Geostationary orbit

Medium Earth orbit

Meteosat
Meteosat is a weather satellite in geostationary orbit. This orbit is special – it means the spacecraft always stays above the same spot on Earth.

HOW SATELLITES WORK //

Satellites must travel at huge speeds to maintain their orbit, but they don't need fuel to keep them going. The rocket that launches the satellite provides the speed, and in space there is nothing to slow the satellite down. Small thrusters allow the satellite to make adjustments to its position. Solar panels provide power for the satellite's equipment.

LAUNCHING A SATELLITE //

Designing and building a satellite can take years, but its journey into space can take as little as ten minutes. A rocket delivers the satellite first into Earth orbit, then onwards to its exact destination. Satellites have their own thrusters, which they can use for this final step in the journey, and to keep themselves in the right position once they get there.

Rocket launch //
The first stage of the rocket gets the spacecraft off the ground and out of Earth's atmosphere. This stage needs the most power as air resistance slows the rocket down.

Second stage and third stages fire //
The second stage gets the spacecraft into Earth orbit, then the third stage engines fire up to deliver it to its intended location.

Satellite separates //
Once in a stable orbit the spacecraft separates from the upper stage of the rocket. The rocket usually falls back to Earth and the spacecraft gets ready to start working.

Satellite unfolds //
The spacecraft unfolds its solar arrays then prepares to start doing its job. The satellite's instruments turn on, and its position and systems are checked.

Landsat 8
A Sun-synchronous orbit means a satellite passes over the same part of Earth at the same time every day. Landsat 8 takes pictures of Earth, so seeing places at the same time every day helps it to look for changes.

RHESSI
Polar orbits pass over the North and South poles. This can be useful to investigate these locations or to give an uninterrupted view of the Sun. RHESSI was a mission in a polar orbit investigating solar flares.

Starlink
Starlink communication satellites contact Earth frequently. Low Earth orbit puts them close so that signals are received quickly.

Global Positioning System (GPS)
The GPS constellation used for satellite navigation is found in medium Earth orbit – close enough to send regular signals but far enough away that not too many satellites are needed to cover the whole planet.

ORBITING EARTH //
Satellites follow a curved path around Earth. We call this path an orbit. Satellites in a low Earth orbit are typically less than 1,000 km (620 miles) from Earth's surface, while those in a highly elliptical orbit can be as far away as 40,000 km (24,800 miles) at their furthest point.

CREWED CRAFT

Fewer than 700 people have ever been to space. Sending humans into space is expensive and risky, and the spacecraft used must not only protect the crew in space, but also bring them home safely. Many crewed missions are for scientific research, but the trend for "space tourism" is also growing.

HUMAN-RATED SPACECRAFT //

A wide range of spacecraft carry humans into space for different missions, but most have a similar shape – a wide circular base, sloping sides, and a blunt-tipped nose cone. This is the best shape to carry the weight of the crew while also withstanding the heat the spacecraft will generate in space, especially during its descent back to Earth.

Soyuz
Russia/Soviet Union (ROSCOSMOS)
First launch: 1966
Size: 2.2 m x 7.2 m (7 ft x 24 ft)

Shenzhou
China (CNSA)
First launch: 1999
Size: 2.2 m x 9.25 m (7 ft x 30 ft)

Crew Dragon
USA (SpaceX)
First launch: 2019
Size: 4 m x 8.1 m (13 ft x 27 ft)

Starliner
USA (Boeing)
First launch: 2019
Size 4.5 m x 5 m (15 ft x 16 ft)

Orion
USA (NASA)
First launch: 2014
Size: 5 m x 3.3 m (16 ft x 11 ft)

Mengzhou
China (CNSA)
First launch: 2020
Size: 4.5 m x 7.2 m (15 ft x 24 ft)

Gaganyaan
India (ISRO)
First launch: targeting 2026
Size: 3.5 m x 3.58 m (11 ft x 12 ft)

Starship
USA (SpaceX)
First Launch: 2023
Full spacecraft size: 9 m x 32 m (30 ft x 105 ft)
Payload bay size: 9 m x 17.2 m (30 ft x 56 ft)

SPACE TOURISM //
People who have very little space training can now go into space. Organizations such as Blue Origin and Virgin Galactic offer trips to the edge of space, which cost at least £450,000 ($600,000) and last about 11 minutes. The New Shepard, seen above, is a reusable suborbital rocket that takes humans to the edge of space where they can experience weightlessness and incredible views of Earth.

COMMERCIAL SPACE FLIGHTS //
The Polaris Dawn mission, launched in 2024, was one of the first to be carried out by a private company, rather than a government agency such as NASA. SpaceX provided the rocket and spacecraft for billionaire businessman Jared Isaacman and his crew to spend six days in space conducting experiments and raising money for charity. They also performed the first ever commercial spacewalk.

Hubble Space Telescope
From its low Earth orbit, 515 km (320 miles) away, Hubble is accessible for maintenance missions, but far enough away to capture amazing images of space.

HUMAN HELPERS //
There are some tasks in space that humans do best. Here, a crew from the Space Shuttle orbiter *Endeavour* perform essential maintenance and repairs on the Hubble Space Telescope during an 11-day mission in December 1993. Launched in 1990, Hubble was only supposed to last for about 15 years, but it is still going strong today, thanks to service missions like this one.

Robotic arm
The Space Shuttle's arm holds astronauts safely while they work on Hubble. It is controlled by crew members inside the orbiter.

Holding steady
Before the crew worked on Hubble, it was grappled by the robotic arm, berthed inside the payload bay, and attached to this platform.

Reaching the top
The robotic arm is about to hoist the astronaut more than 13 m (43 ft) to the top of Hubble to install protective covers onto the magnetometers.

DISCOVERY //
Six Shuttle orbiters were built for flight: *Enterprise, Columbia, Challenger, Discovery, Atlantis,* and *Endeavour.* Each of them made multiple flights but *Discovery* flew the most at 39 missions. In this image it is taking off from Kennedy Space Center in 2007. The mission delivered four bedrooms to the International Space Station in a module called Harmony.

External tank
This huge tank carried all the liquid hydrogen and oxygen the Space Shuttle used as fuel. Its orange colour came from the spray-on insulation in which it was covered.

Lightning rod
This fibreglass mast stood 24 m (80 ft) high, protecting the rocket and service structure from lightning strikes.

Solid booster
The two solid rocket boosters separated from the Shuttle after about two minutes. They would fall into the sea and be recovered by two boats.

Iconic orbiter
The orbiter launched vertically, its three engines supplied with liquid fuel from the external tank.

SPACE SHUTTLE

First launched in 1981, the Space Shuttle was a very unusual rocket system. Its plane-shaped orbiter launched vertically but could glide back to Earth after a mission to be refuelled and reused. Shuttle flew 133 times carrying more than 350 people into space before being decommissioned in 2011. It was involved in many missions including launching the Hubble Space Telescope and building the International Space Station.

SPACE PLANE //
In space, the orbiter flew like a spacecraft. The crew module was at the front of the craft, with the large payload bay in the mid-section, big enough to fit a small bus inside. Once in space the doors would open up and satellites and equipment could be released into space. Shuttle *Atlantis* is seen here over the Bahamas with its payload bay doors open.

TOUCHDOWN //
To return to Earth, the orbiter passed back into Earth's atmosphere belly-first. Special black insulation tiles on the underside stopped it from getting too hot as friction from the atmosphere slowed it down. It then glided in big, swooping S-shapes to slow down even further. Finally, the orbiter touched down on a long runway, using parachutes to bring it to a halt.

DOCKING WITH THE ISS

Larger than a six-bedroom house, the International Space Station (ISS) is a mobile science lab that orbits Earth at an altitude of around 400 km (250 miles). It can house seven crew members while reaching speeds of 28,000 km/h (17,500 mph). Astronauts travel to the ISS inside spacecraft that are launched via rockets and then dock at the ISS. When it's time to go home, the spacecraft are undocked and make the journey back to Earth.

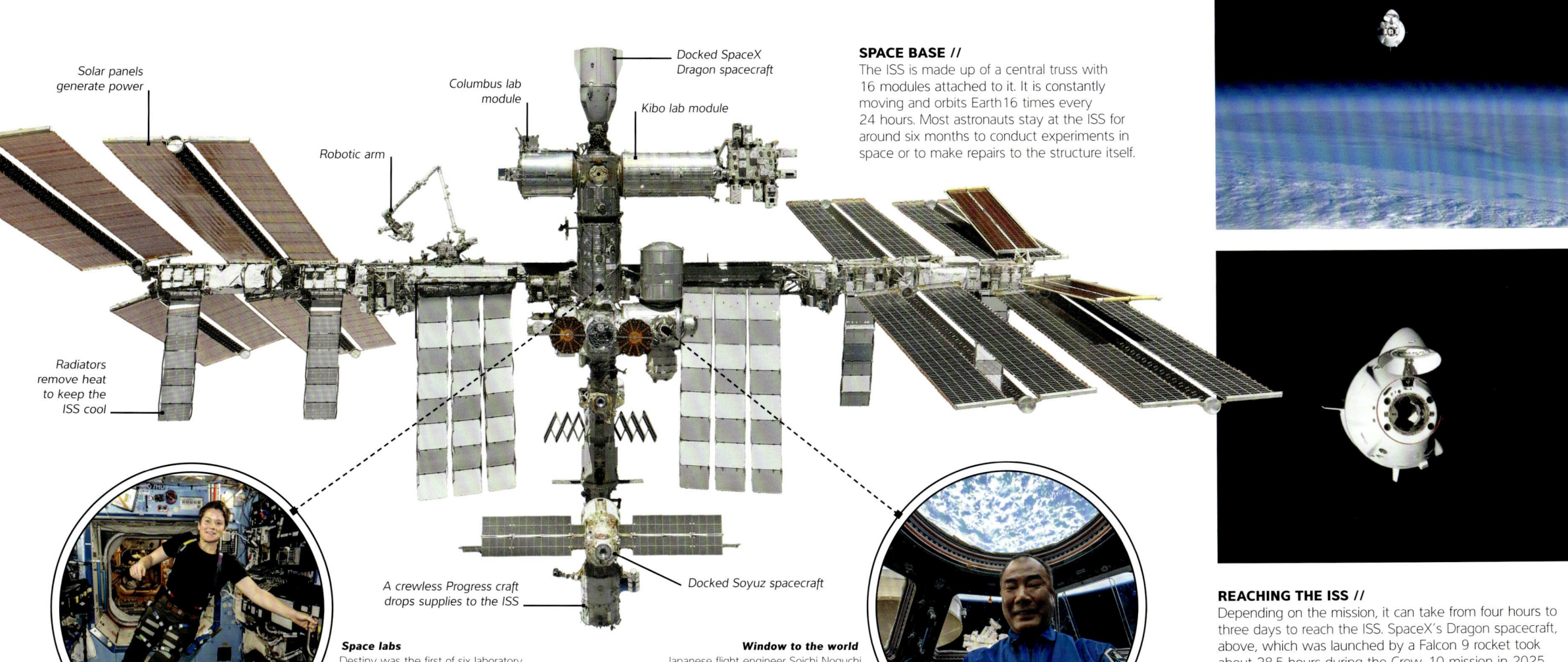

Solar panels generate power

Robotic arm

Columbus lab module

Docked SpaceX Dragon spacecraft

Kibo lab module

SPACE BASE //
The ISS is made up of a central truss with 16 modules attached to it. It is constantly moving and orbits Earth 16 times every 24 hours. Most astronauts stay at the ISS for around six months to conduct experiments in space or to make repairs to the structure itself.

Radiators remove heat to keep the ISS cool

A crewless Progress craft drops supplies to the ISS

Docked Soyuz spacecraft

Space labs
Destiny was the first of six laboratory modules to be added to the ISS. Launched in 2001, it is managed by the US. Here, US astronaut Anne McClain is wearing a device that measures her exposure to radiation.

Window to the world
Japanese flight engineer Soichi Noguchi has an incredible view of the Atlantic Ocean through the space station's cupola. This observation deck is made up of six side windows and a large overhead window.

REACHING THE ISS //
Depending on the mission, it can take from four hours to three days to reach the ISS. SpaceX's Dragon spacecraft, above, which was launched by a Falcon 9 rocket took about 28.5 hours during the Crew-10 mission in 2025. As it approaches the ISS, the spacecraft opens its nose cone to reveal the docking port.

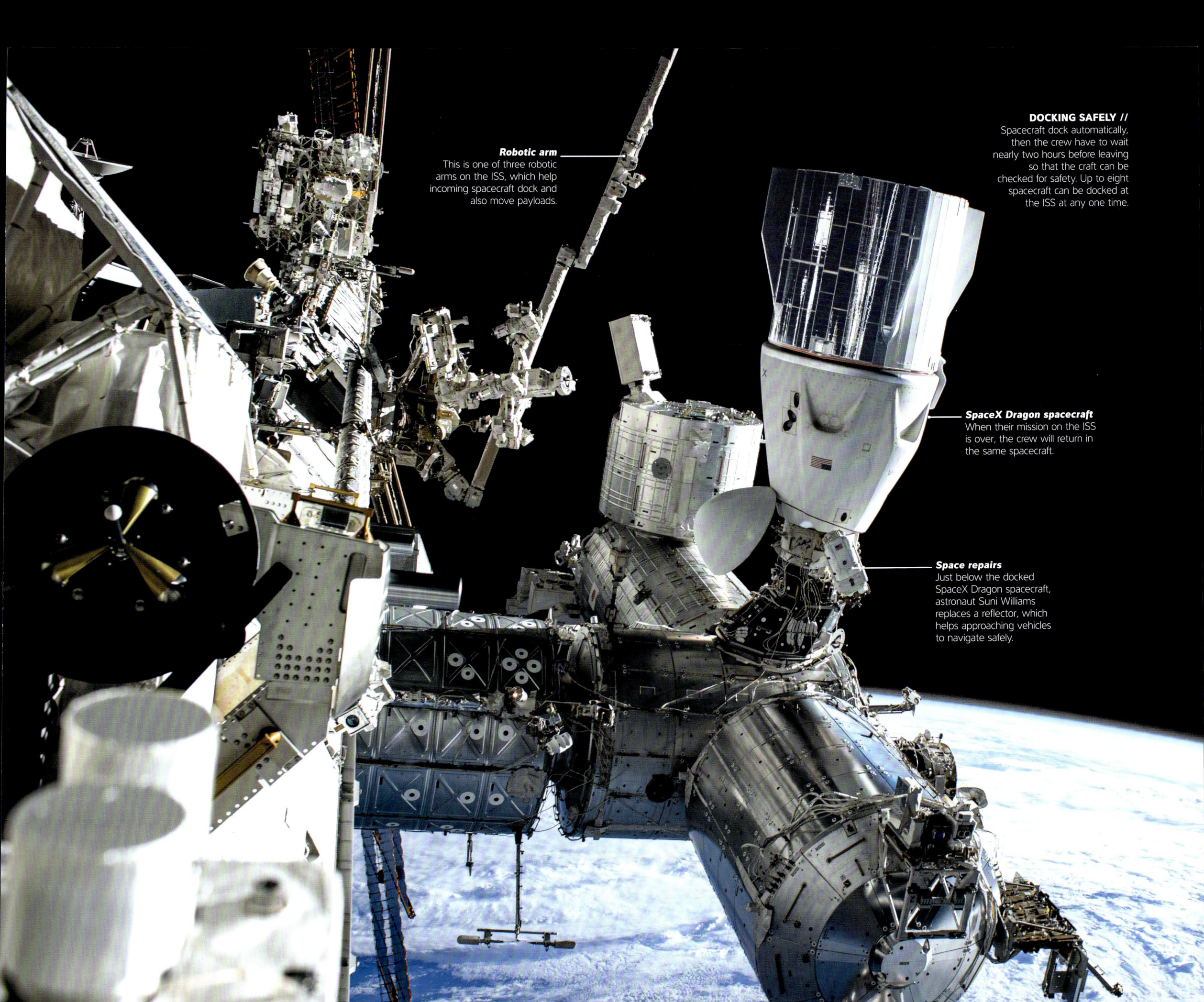

Robotic arm
This is one of three robotic arms on the ISS, which help incoming spacecraft dock and also move payloads.

DOCKING SAFELY //
Spacecraft dock automatically, then the crew have to wait nearly two hours before leaving so that the craft can be checked for safety. Up to eight spacecraft can be docked at the ISS at any one time.

SpaceX Dragon spacecraft
When their mission on the ISS is over, the crew will return in the same spacecraft.

Space repairs
Just below the docked SpaceX Dragon spacecraft, astronaut Suni Williams replaces a reflector, which helps approaching vehicles to navigate safely.

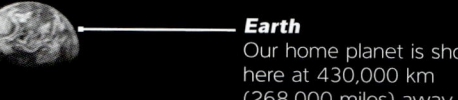

Earth
Our home planet is shown here at 430,000 km (268,000 miles) away from the Orion spacecraft.

FAR FROM HOME //

This image was taken during the Artemis I mission, showing the Orion spacecraft at the furthest point in its orbit with both Earth and the Moon visible in the background. The spacecraft has an external camera attached to each of its four solar arrays, which is how this selfie was snapped. The cameras also allow NASA engineers to inspect the outside of the spacecraft while it is in flight.

Crew module
This part of the spacecraft is where up to four astronauts will sit for launch and where they will live during the journey to the Moon.

Service module
From fuel tanks to thruster systems, all the equipment to keep the spacecraft working is kept in this module.

SPACE LAUNCH SYSTEM

One of the most famous achievements of humanity's space exploration was visiting the Moon in the 1960s and '70s. Now NASA is aiming to return humans to the Moon, using the new Space Launch System (SLS) rocket. As part of the Artemis missions, the SLS rocket is designed to carry the Orion spacecraft beyond Earth's orbit and into deep space.

SPACE LAUNCH SYSTEM ROCKET //
Standing at 98 m (321 ft) tall, the SLS is a super-heavy-lift rocket made up of an enormous core stage with four RS-25 engines and two solid rocket boosters. The Orion spacecraft attaches to an upper stage powered by a single engine. At launch it is 15 per cent more powerful than the Saturn V rocket used during the Apollo missions almost 50 years earlier.

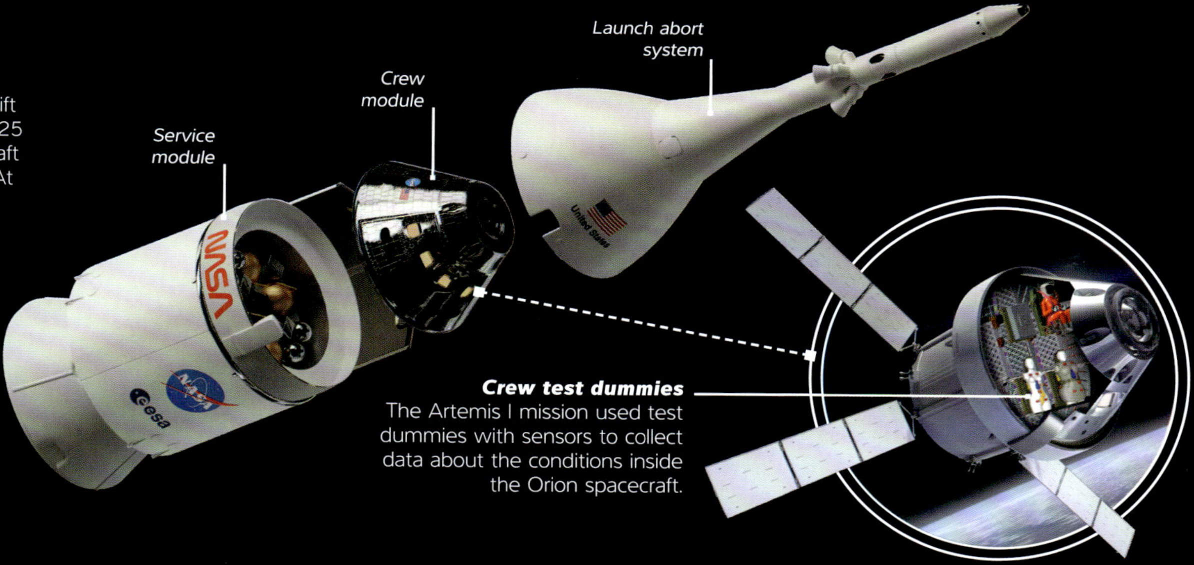

Service module

Crew module

Launch abort system

Crew test dummies
The Artemis I mission used test dummies with sensors to collect data about the conditions inside the Orion spacecraft.

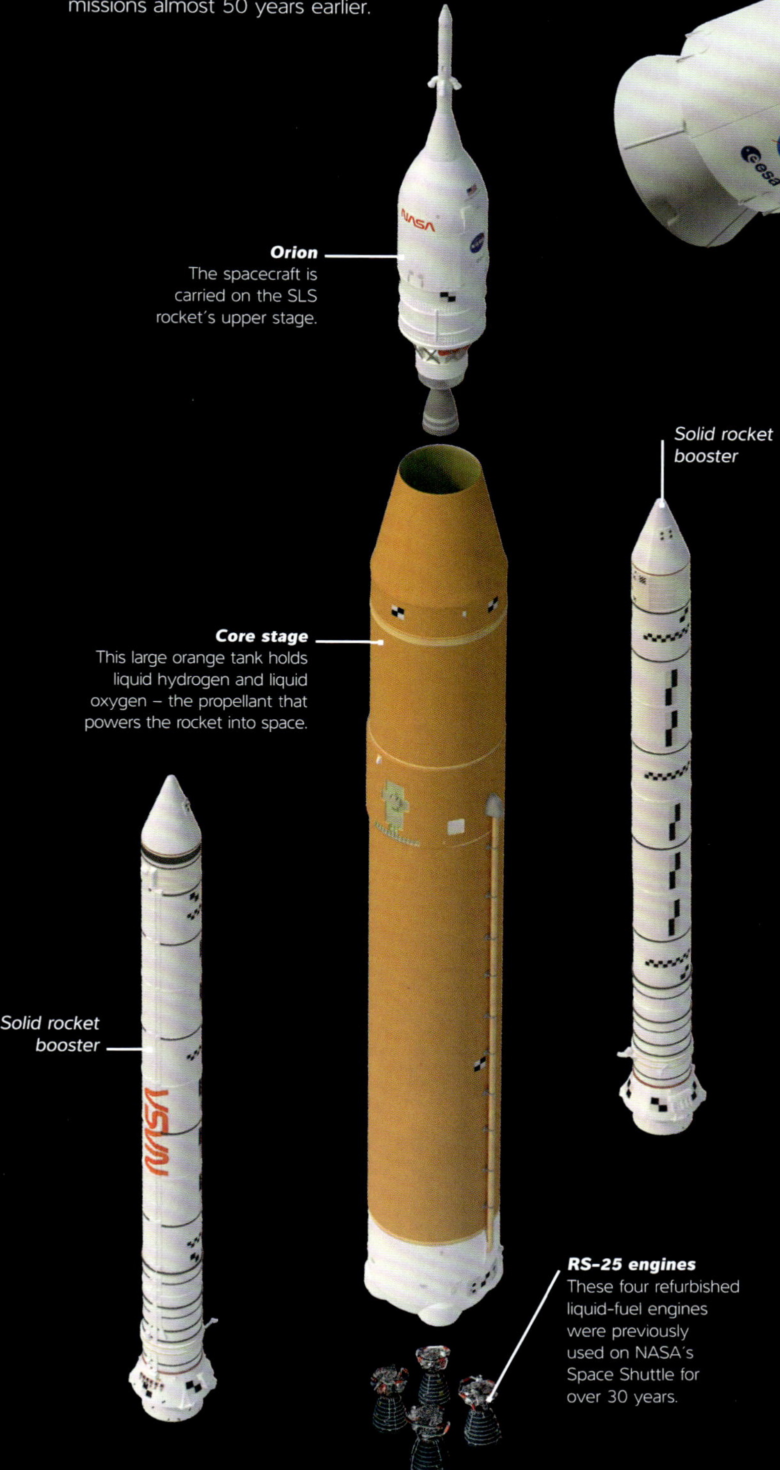

Orion
The spacecraft is carried on the SLS rocket's upper stage.

Solid rocket booster

Core stage
This large orange tank holds liquid hydrogen and liquid oxygen – the propellant that powers the rocket into space.

Solid rocket booster

RS-25 engines
These four refurbished liquid-fuel engines were previously used on NASA's Space Shuttle for over 30 years.

ARTEMIS PROGRAM //

NASA's Artemis Program aims to return humans to the Moon, and eventually build a permanent base there. Artemis I was an uncrewed mission that orbited the Moon. Artemis II will take four astronauts around the Moon, while Artemis III aims to land astronauts at the Moon's South Pole.

Artemis I launch
In November 2022, NASA's SLS rocket carrying the Orion spacecraft launched on the first Artemis mission. Lifting off from the Kennedy Space Center in Florida, USA, this uncrewed test flight flew around the Moon and returned to Earth in 25 days, travelling over 2.2 million km (1.4 million miles).

MIGHTY SATURN V

The Saturn V was one of the most powerful rockets ever built. Developed by NASA in the 1960s, this incredible feat of engineering stood 111 m (364 ft) tall and was designed with the main goal of delivering people to the surface of the Moon as part of the Apollo program. It successfully launched 13 times: two of these were test launches, 10 were Apollo flights, while the final Saturn V mission in 1973 launched NASA's first space station, Skylab.

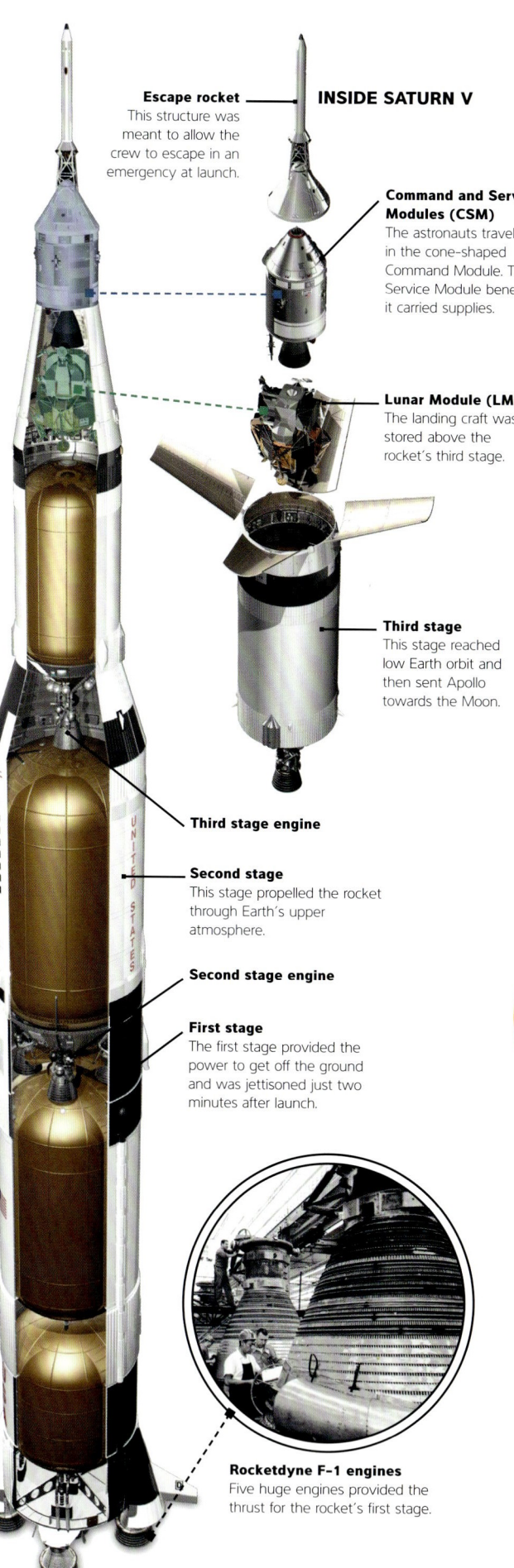

INSIDE SATURN V

Escape rocket — This structure was meant to allow the crew to escape in an emergency at launch.

Command and Service Modules (CSM) — The astronauts travelled in the cone-shaped Command Module. The Service Module beneath it carried supplies.

Lunar Module (LM) — The landing craft was stored above the rocket's third stage.

Third stage — This stage reached low Earth orbit and then sent Apollo towards the Moon.

Third stage engine

Second stage — This stage propelled the rocket through Earth's upper atmosphere.

Second stage engine

First stage — The first stage provided the power to get off the ground and was jettisoned just two minutes after launch.

Rocketdyne F-1 engines — Five huge engines provided the thrust for the rocket's first stage.

APOLLO 11 ASTRONAUTS //
Neil Armstrong, Buzz Aldrin, and Michael Collins are seen here as they prepare to board Apollo 11. In total, 24 Apollo astronauts rode the Saturn V. It was the first rocket to take people beyond low Earth orbit and enabled 12 of them to set foot on the surface of the Moon.

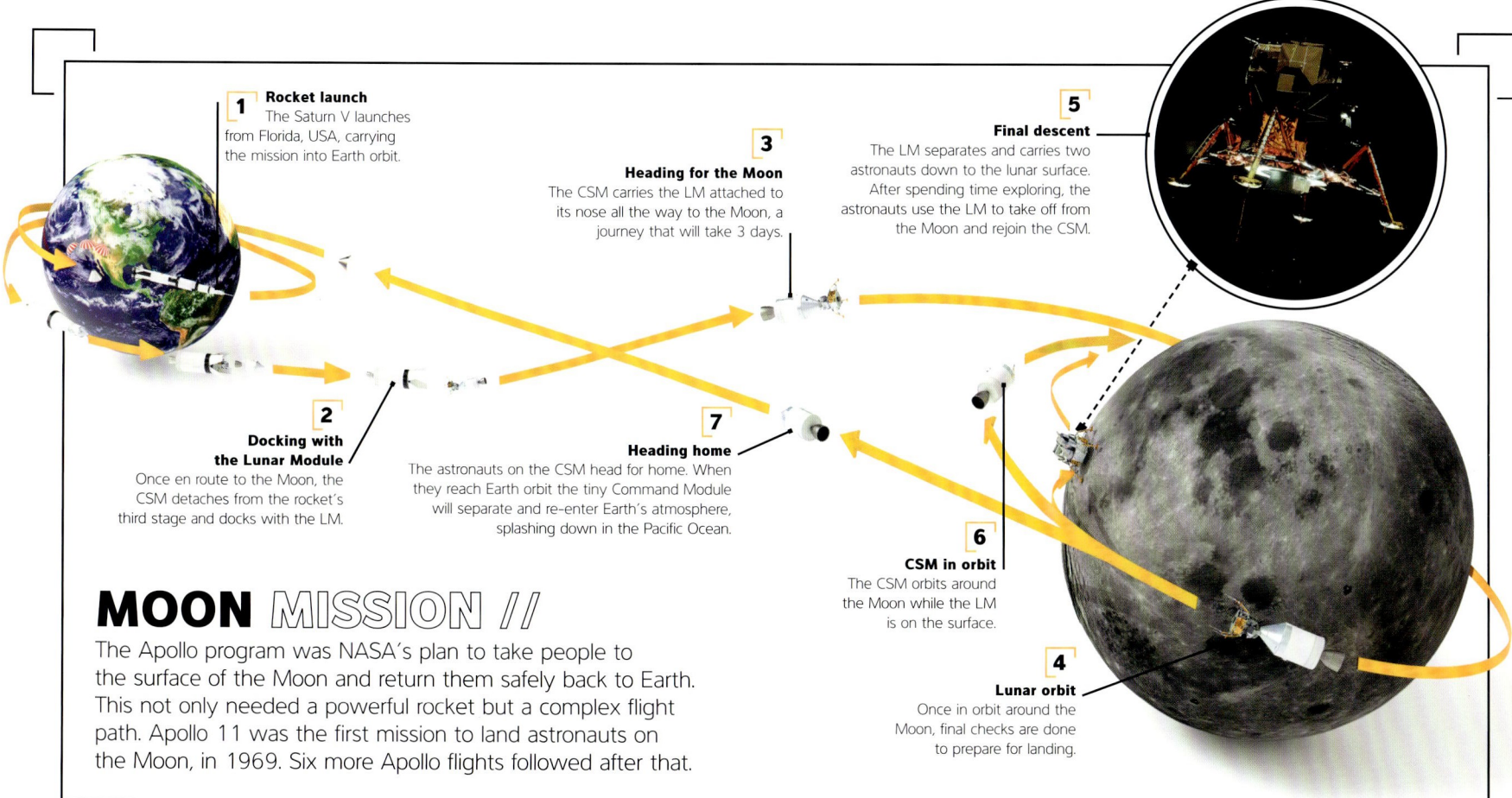

MOON MISSION //

The Apollo program was NASA's plan to take people to the surface of the Moon and return them safely back to Earth. This not only needed a powerful rocket but a complex flight path. Apollo 11 was the first mission to land astronauts on the Moon, in 1969. Six more Apollo flights followed after that.

1 Rocket launch — The Saturn V launches from Florida, USA, carrying the mission into Earth orbit.

2 Docking with the Lunar Module — Once en route to the Moon, the CSM detaches from the rocket's third stage and docks with the LM.

3 Heading for the Moon — The CSM carries the LM attached to its nose all the way to the Moon, a journey that will take 3 days.

4 Lunar orbit — Once in orbit around the Moon, final checks are done to prepare for landing.

5 Final descent — The LM separates and carries two astronauts down to the lunar surface. After spending time exploring, the astronauts use the LM to take off from the Moon and rejoin the CSM.

6 CSM in orbit — The CSM orbits around the Moon while the LM is on the surface.

7 Heading home — The astronauts on the CSM head for home. When they reach Earth orbit the tiny Command Module will separate and re-enter Earth's atmosphere, splashing down in the Pacific Ocean.

LAUNCH OF APOLLO 11 //
This sequence shows the Saturn V as it clears the launch tower and rises into the sky. The arm of the service tower swings back as the rocket blasts off. During take-off the rocket could be heard more than 64 km (40 miles) away!

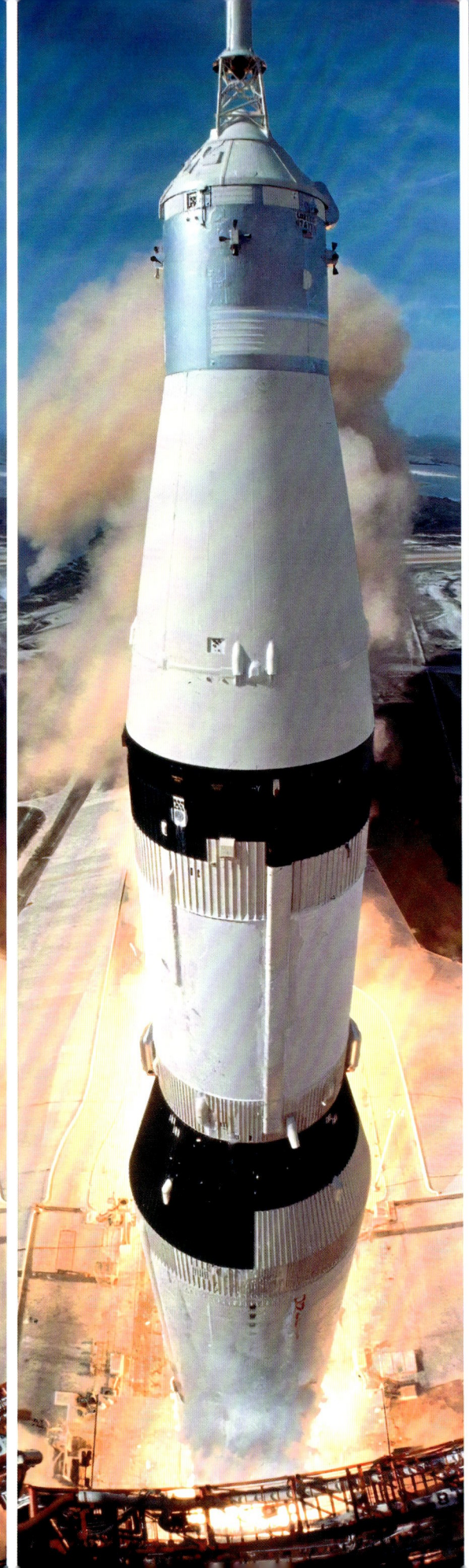

RETURNING HOME

After completing a mission, some uncrewed spacecraft must make the trip back to Earth – if they are carrying samples from asteroids, comets, or the Moon for example. But most often this stage of a mission is seen in crewed flights, when it is time for intrepid astronauts to come home.

RE-ENTRY //

A returning spacecraft goes through a fiery phase called re-entry when it hits Earth's atmosphere. The gases in the atmosphere drag against the craft, which is travelling at enormous speeds, generating huge amounts of heat. The spacecraft must enter the atmosphere at exactly the right angle or it will be destroyed.

SPLASHDOWN
AT SEA //

Many spacecraft come down in the sea. Water provides a slightly softer landing as it absorbs some of the force of impact, making it gentler on the crew or cargo. Since spacecraft landings cannot be highly accurate, the large open space of the sea presents less risk if a re-entry goes slightly off course.

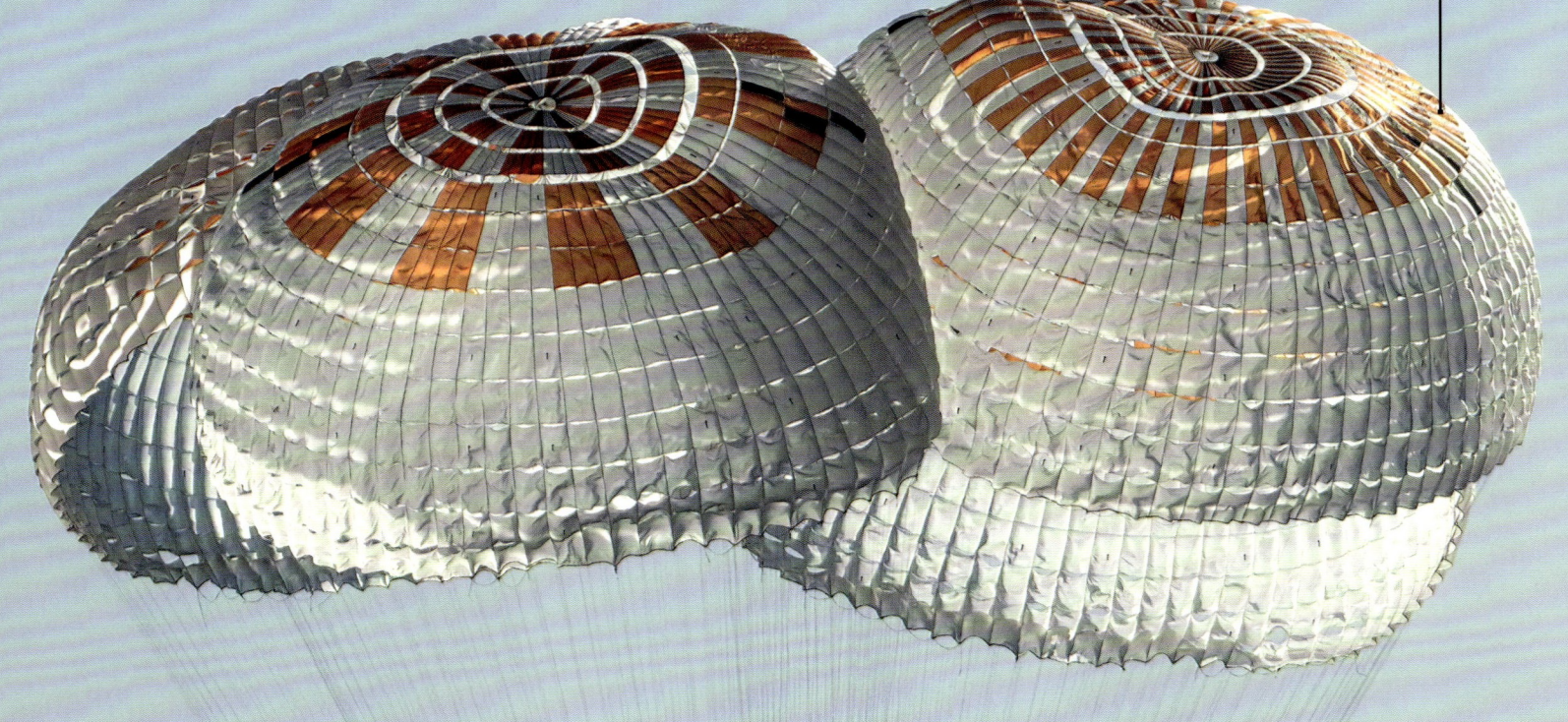

Billowing canopies
Parachutes open during the final stage of the spacecraft's descent, slowing the capsule to a safe speed.

Bumpy landing
Even a watery landing is rough. Astronauts have described being "thrown around" as they arrive back to Earth.

SEA DRAGON //
This is the final touchdown of the SpaceX Crew-4 mission in October 2022. The spacecraft and its crew spent 6 months docked to the ISS before splashing down off the coast of Florida. Once recovered, the capsule was repaired and has since been to space two more times.

RECOVERY CREW //
Support teams are ready to secure the capsule and get the crew and cargo out safely. The first ground crew to reach the spacecraft arrive on fast boats and attach rigging to lift it onto the main recovery vessel.

RECOVERY SHIP //
The capsule is hoisted onto a recovery ship named the *Shannon*. The crane that hoists the capsule is at the back of the vessel, which also contains a medical bay and a helipad in case of emergencies.

TOUCHDOWN ON LAND //

Landing at sea isn't the only option. The Soyuz spacecraft was designed to land in the deserts of Kazakhstan. While providing a slightly rougher landing, the site is much closer to the Soyuz launch facilities, making it easier to get the crew and equipment home. As reusable rocket technology improves, land-based touchdowns of rocket boosters are also becoming more common (see page 39).

Returning to Earth //
The Shenzhou-17 spacecraft is seen here after touchdown in China's Gobi Desert in 2024. After some time in space astronauts are often weakened and can be disoriented. The return crew help them out of the spacecraft to medical facilities, where they are checked over and can start readjusting to being back on Earth.

Soyuz touches down in the desert //
A Soyuz spacecraft touches down in Kazakhstan on 7 September 2016. Moments before the capsule touches the ground it fires its retro-rocket motors. These provide a force that slows the capsule just before touchdown to ensure the landing is safe.

LAUNCH VEHICLES

The first rocket ever to launch a payload into orbit was the USSR's Sputnik, which sent the world's first satellite into space in 1957. Since then, many countries have built launch vehicles that can reach orbit. These pages show some notable examples, arranged in order of size.

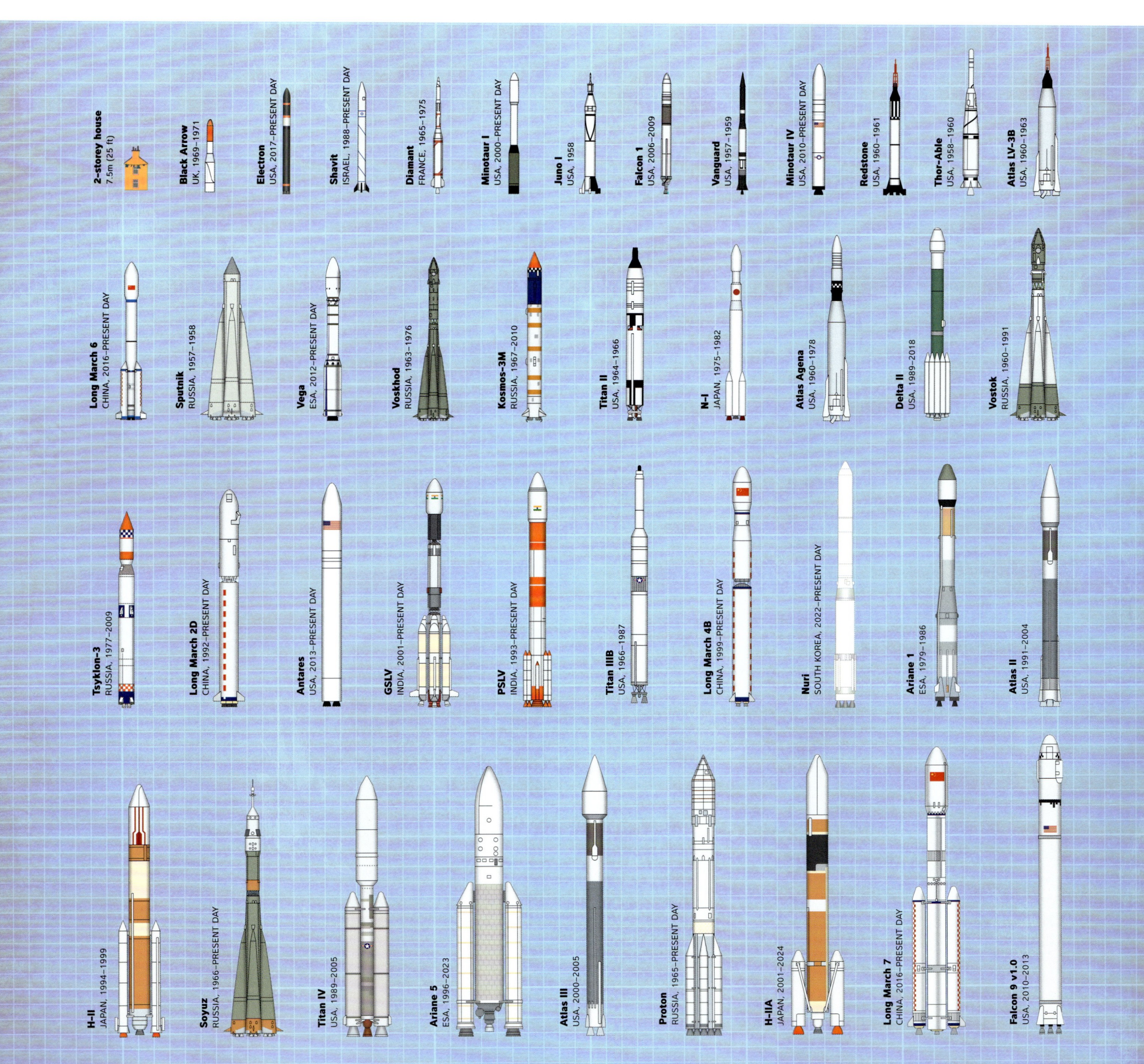

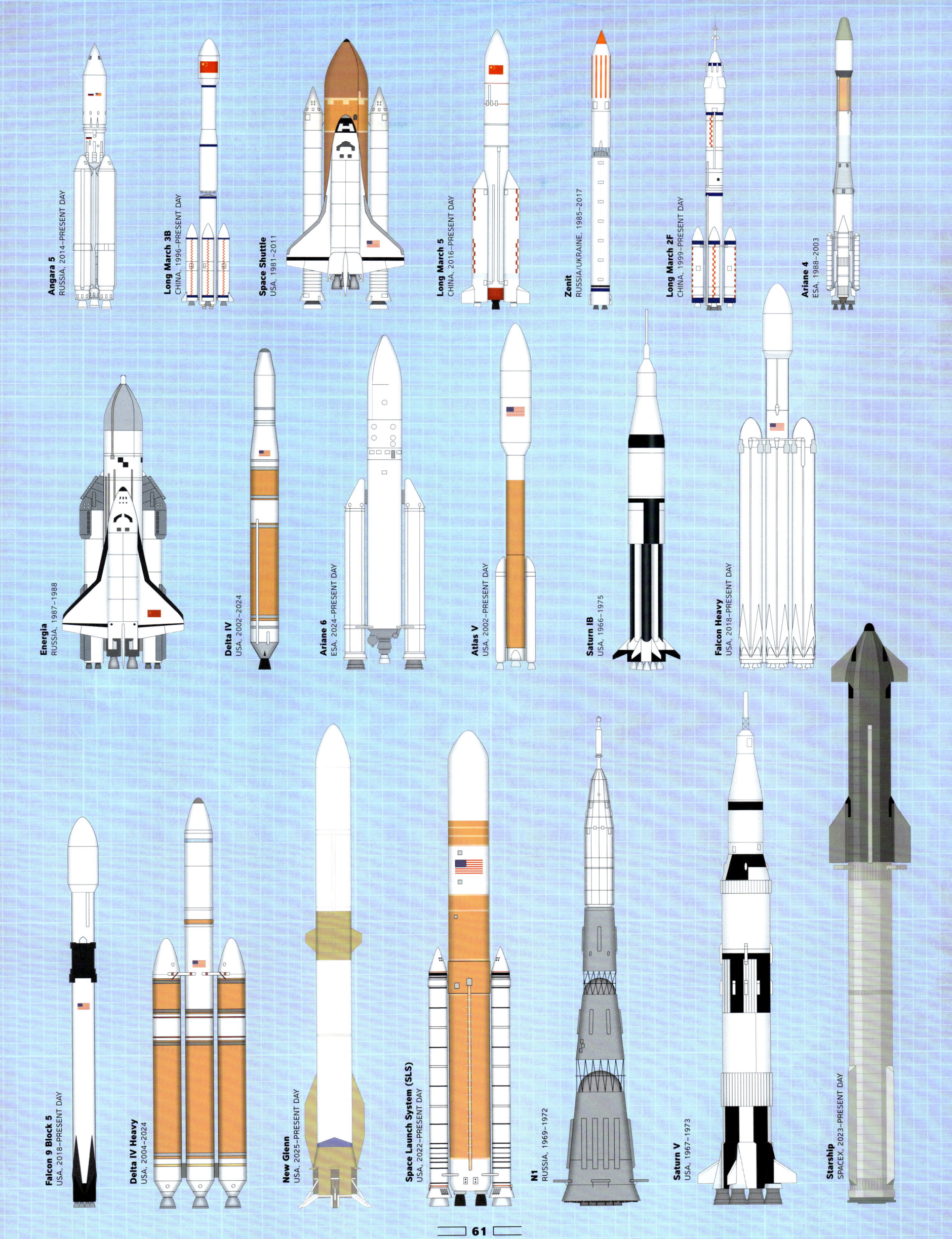

PACIFIC SPACEPORT COMPLEX, USA //
Opened in 1998, this launch site on Kodiak Island, Alaska, is used for both government and private launches of small rockets. Its two launch pads have been used for more than 30 missions, including satellites launches.

VANDENBERG SPACE FORCE BASE, USA //
What began as a Californian army base to train soldiers became this rocket launch site in the 1950s. Since then it has been the main launch facility for Delta and Atlas rockets.

CAPE CANAVERAL SPACE FORCE STATION AND THE KENNEDY SPACE CENTER, USA //
These two sites are very close to one another in Florida, USA. Cape Canaveral is run by the US military, while the Kennedy Space Center has been NASA's main launch site since 1968.

CORN RANCH, USA //
This spaceport in Texas, USA, is home to the Blue Origin space company. They offer sub-orbital space flights (a short journey into space and back again that lasts a few minutes) for paying explorers. So far around 60 space tourists have flown on missions launched from this site.

LAUNCH SITES

There are many rocket launch sites around the world. Also called spaceports, they usually have a range of facilities including a launch pad, control centre, and fuel storage. Most launch sites are close to the sea or deserts to reduce the risk of debris falling over areas where people live.

SPACEX STARBASE, USA //
Home to two of the world's tallest launch towers, Starbase in Texas, USA, is the main launch and test facility for SpaceX's Starship rocket. It has two launch pads, a mission control facility, a Starship rocket factory, and even homes for some of the team to live on site.

GUIANA SPACE CENTRE, FRENCH GUIANA //
Located in South America, this centre is also called Europe's Spaceport because it is used for space launches carried out by the European Space Agency. Launching near to the equator, where Earth's rotation is fastest, gives rockets an extra boost.

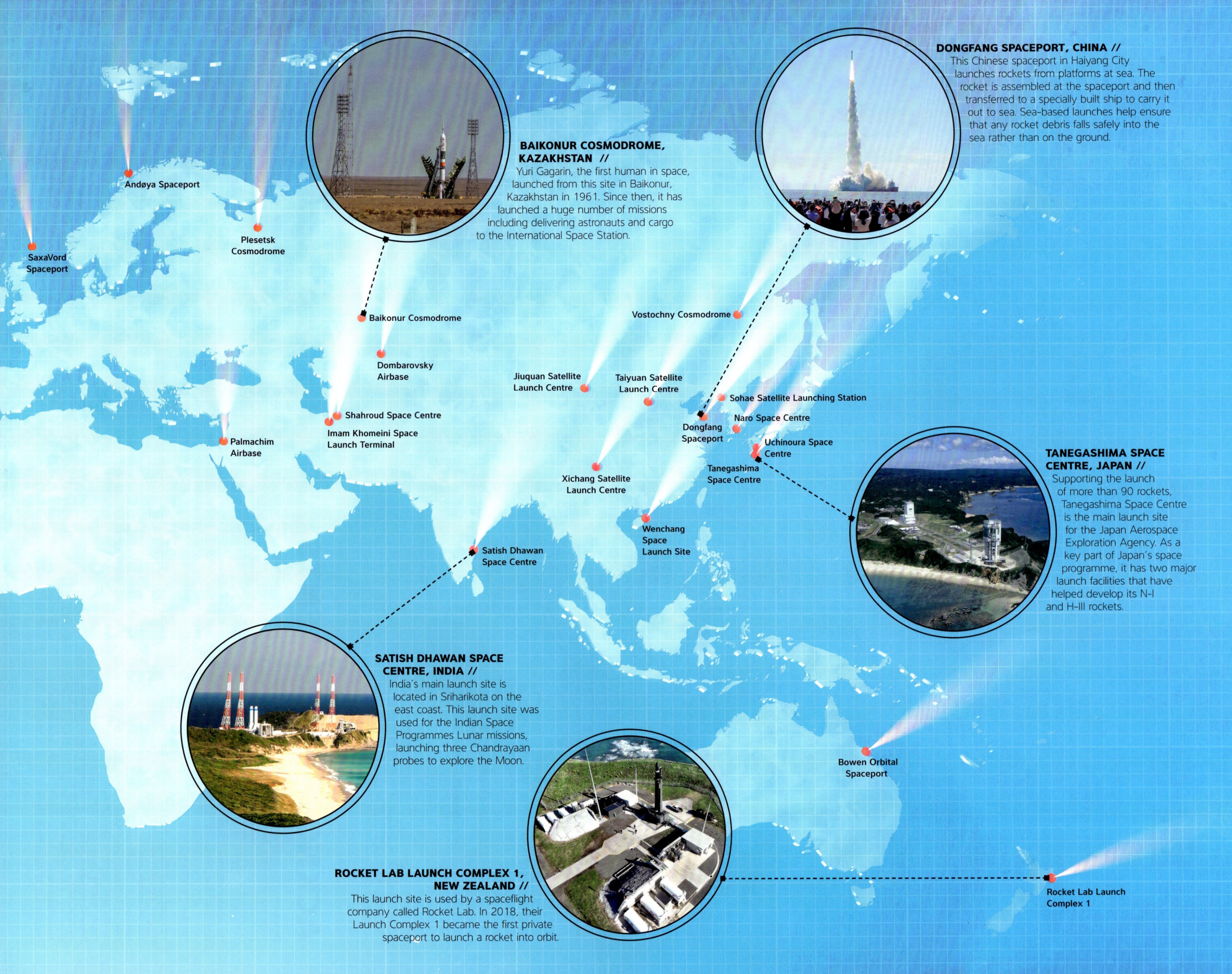